IE FOR THE SHOP FLOOR

Productivity Through Process Analysis

IE FOR THE SHOP FLOOR

Productivity Through Process Analysis

Junichi Ishiwata

Foreword by
Gifford M. Brown
Ford Motor Company

Publisher's Message by
Norman Bodek
President, Productivity, Inc.

Productivity Press, Inc.
Cambridge, Massachusetts   Norwalk, Connecticut

Originally published as *Gemba no IE (I): kōtei bunseki (Worksite IE (I): Process analysis)*, Volume 9 in the *Gemba QC dokuhon (New worksite QC primer)* series compiled by the *QC Circle* magazine editorial group and published by JUSE Press, Ltd., 1984, 1988. Copyright © 1984 Junichi Ishiwata.

English translation copyright © 1991 Productivity Press, Inc. Translated by Bruce Talbot. English translation arranged with JUSE Press, Ltd., Tokyo, through Japan Foreign-Rights Centre.

Productivity Press
P.O. Box 3007
Cambridge, Massachusetts 02140
United States of America
Telephone: (617) 497-5146
Telefax: (617) 868-3524

Cover design by David B. Lennon
Typeset by Productivity Press
Printed and bound by BookCrafters
Printed in the United States of America
Printed on acid-free paper

Library of Congress Cataloging-in-Publication Data

Ishiwata, Junichi.
    [Genba no IE. English]
    IE for the shop floor / cJunichi Ishiwata ; [translated by Bruce Talbot].
    2 v. ; cm.
    Translation of: Genba no IE.
    Vol. 2 written by Katō Ken'ichirō.
    Contents: 1. Productivity through process analysis — 2. Productivity through motion study.
    ISBN 0-915299-82-8 (v. 1) — ISBN 1-56327-000-5 (v. 2).
    1. Factory management.   2. Production control.   3. Quality circles.
I. Katō, Ken'ichirō, 1947- . II. Title.
TS155.I7313   1991   91-2193
670.4--dc20   CIP

    92 93 10 9 8 7 6 5 4 3 2

Contents

Publisher's Message

It is a pleasure to present *Productivity Through Process Analysis*, the first volume of a four-part set, *IE for the Shop Floor*.

Since their "discovery" by Frederick Taylor, the Gilbreths, and other early pioneers, industrial engineering methods in manufacturing plants have improved productivity tremendously over the years. Ford Motor was one of the early experimenters. Using IE methods in the first part of this century, the Ford production system was able to double the output of automobiles — and double the wages of the workers.

The focal point of industrial engineering is the improvement of productivity. Using IE and quality improvement methodologies, Western companies have made enormous strides in the past. Traditionally, these tools were placed in the hands of specialists. Professional engineers and managers were often the exclusive decision makers in these issues, despite the inherent expertise of the shop floor people who did the job every day and best knew the situation. Management rarely asked these workers for their improvement ideas or trained them in ways to analyze the situation.

Today we know there has to be a different approach to the improvement of quality and productivity. Over the last 10 to 12 years, we have seen the difference in results of companies in which only specialists can make a change, and those in which every individual, from the CEO to the newest hourly worker, is committed to continuous improvement. The Japanese have shown us that we can't afford not to involve every member of the company in this drive. *Everyone* in the company must be aware that he or she can make a difference in the vitality of the company — and must be educated, given the tools, and empowered to make that difference.

Industrial engineering is a complex science that has developed in great depth and in a number of diverse yet related directions. Yet from this detailed knowledge, a set of simple and effective techniques can be extracted and applied directly to improve work in manufacturing plants.

The unique value of this set of books is its accessible approach to the material. They were not written for engineers in offices far removed from the production line, but rather for the training of supervisors and workers right where the action is — on the shop floor.

With the new audience for these methods comes a new frame of reference about how they can be used. These books are not about work analysis methods as a management control tool. This is industrial engineering for the workers themselves to use. It is participative, employee-involved IE.

The approach described in these books is rooted in an understanding of the value of *kaizen*, or continuous improvement. To successfully compete on quality, cost, and delivery, large-scale innovation is simply not enough. The world's leading manufacturing companies are ahead today because their employees — from the executive suite to the drafting room to the shop floor — are constantly fine-tuning their processes and looking for even small ways to improve the work.

You are probably familiar with many of the tools of kaizen — improvement teams have been using the 7 QC Tools, the 7 New Tools, and related methods for years. With this set, four basic IE methods join the tool kit to increase the range of improvement possibilities.

Process analysis is a method for visualizing on paper the individual steps in a process, then working to eliminate unnecessary or wasteful ones, such as transportation or delays. The aim is to shorten and streamline processes, saving time and cost to better serve the customer.

Productivity Through Process Analysis gives a thorough introduction to process analysis as a bottom-up work improvement method, teaching how to prepare process analysis charts and process diagrams. Separate chapters describe specific applications such as product and operator process analysis, joint analysis of several operators or operator plus machine, and analysis of the administrative processes that accompany production. The book is rounded out with case studies reporting shop floor improvements that were made using these methods, with three full-length case presentations in the final chapter.

We hope that these powerful techniques become part of your company's competitive advantage in the hands of your supervisors and team leaders.

I would like to express my thanks to the author, Junichi Ishiwata, for his clear expression of the subject of process analysis, to Zenichiro Kurita, president of JUSE Press, and to Katsuharu Arai, director of the editorial department of JUSE Press, for permitting us to translate these valuable books. I am also grateful to Akira Kashima of the Japan Foreign-Rights Centre for facilitating the publishing arrangements. We especially thank Gifford Brown, manager of Ford Motor's Cleveland Engine Plants and a pacesetter in manufacturing process improvement, for contributing a fine foreword to the book. Steven Ott, vice president and general manager of Productivity Press, has my appreciation for producing these English editions.

A special thanks to the many people who helped produce these books: to Bruce Talbot, for his fine translation; to Karen Jones for editorial development of the text and figures; to Mugi Hanao for special editorial assistance with translation questions; to Marie Cantlon and Dorothy Lohmann for managing the manuscript editing, with the assistance of Christine Carvajal (copyediting), Leslie Macmillan (word processing), Aurelia Navarro (proofreading), and Jennifer Cross (indexing); to David Lennon for managing the production of the book and designing the covers; and to Gayle Joyce, Susan Cobb, Jane Donovan, Gary Ragaglia, Michelle Seery, and Karla Tolbert for typesetting and the professional preparation of the illustrations.

Norman Bodek
President
Productivity, Inc.

Foreword

The accelerating complexities of modern organizations demand new dimensions in modern management. Perhaps the most profound and promising of these dimensions is the emerging utilization of process analysis in successfully achieving *kaizen* or continuous improvement.

As a plant manager, I have been involved in the successful implementation of process analysis in a manufacturing environment. In the past, we were comfortable with the success of our manufacturing processes, even though we had problems of waste, irrationality, and inconsistency, which the Japanese refer to as the "Big 3." Global competition has focused attention on our manufacturing inefficiencies and motivated us to improve our processes.

The Japanese have made continuous improvements over the years in small incremental steps. Western organizations sometimes perceive that the Japanese competitive lead in quality and productivity is based on quantum technological leaps. In reality, however, much of the Japanese success is based on continuous improvement through all levels of the organization.

As Ford strives to become more competitive in the global market, there has been intense pressure to make our plants more competitive. The magnitude of the problems associated with the old manufacturing methods required a change in the culture at all levels of the organization. Changing the culture was difficult, due to the diversified interest of the groups involved in the decision-making process, including various unions, trades, plants, suppliers, and the workforce.

In order to get the cooperation of these groups, a win-win situation had to be developed. Our long-term future is directly related to our quality, productivity, efficiency, and attitude. Our accomplishments are constantly being compared with our competitors on a global scale. In this age of declining volumes and capital expenditures, our plants have been forced to become more efficient. We have chosen to improve our global competitiveness through the use of continuous improvement methodologies.

We slowly opened the kaizen "umbrella" — which included total productive maintenance (TPM), zero defects, small group activities (employee involvement), cooperative labor-management relations, and elements of Total Quality Excellence — by developing offshoots of these programs designed for the Ford environment. These programs originated with the company-wide implementation of statistical process control (SPC), a program extensively utilized by the Japanese in the early 1960s. In the same way, we want to implement process analysis through all levels of the organization. The process of locking the kaizen umbrella in its open position has been the implementation of process analysis.

Our success with these programs is based on the cooperation and buy-in of all members of the workforce, including managers, and salaried and hourly personnel. Process analysis may sound difficult, but it really is not. All levels of an organization can learn the simple techniques as part of their improvement activities.

Process analysis is a fundamental ingredient of continuous improvement. It is a method of obtaining useful data required to improve quality, reduce non-value added work, and maintain continuous improvement. The system makes extensive use of individual creative ideas and the analysis of facts, coupled with numerous problem-solving tools, including process analysis charts, flow diagrams, data summary charts, PQCDSM and 5W1H checklists, and Pareto charts. This book describes in detail how to use these tools in the various applications of process analysis.

The American auto industry has driven itself to adopt various quality and improvement programs. Many other industries that are not facing similar competitive pressures are missing a major opportunity to make a positive effect on the bottom line. Organizations often tend to be overwhelmed by the energy needed to promote a cultural change. Nevertheless, a proactive approach will make any activity less vulnerable to future economic and competitive demands. This is particularly true in the world today, where it is difficult to raise prices sufficiently to offset rising costs. Continuous improvement supported by process analysis enables the company to improve efficiencies and thereby increase profit margins.

This book is a practical and informative guide for all levels of factory and office personnel in using process analysis and industrial engineering techniques to improve quality and productivity. I encourage you to consider how your entire workforce might put these ideas to use in your organization.

Gifford M. Brown
Plant Manager
Cleveland Engine Plants
Ford Motor Company

Preface

In the 20-plus years of QC circle activities in Japan, we have seen the QC circle movement spread far and wide. The means used by QC circle members to resolve quality issues have been centered on the seven QC tools and other QC methods but have also included various conventional industrial engineering (IE) techniques.

Much of the success enjoyed by Japanese manufacturing industries can be traced to factories that benefit from QC circle activities. However, to overcome the challenges of today's highly competitive business environment, manufacturers cannot afford to rest on their laurels but must achieve even higher levels of quality control. Today, technical progress is so rapid that companies that stand still are, in effect, moving backward. Companies that hope to survive not only must provide goods or services that satisfy customers, they must do so quickly and cheaply. Once we realize this, we rightly see factories as a vital key to success, and we recognize the endless need for improvement. In the future, the successful factories will be the ones that do not passively wait for problems to occur but work actively to predict problems and solve them before they occur. To do this, they should use IE techniques to identify problems and make improvements.

This book is part of the *New Worksite QC Primer* series published by JUSE Press and is one of four books based on IE-related themes.* The theme of this book is process analysis. Naturally, process analysis is related in various ways to other IE techniques (such as those for motion study, conveyance and equipment layout, and time study), and I suggest that readers study all four of the IE-related books in the series. Nevertheless, readers who are interested specifically in process analysis will find this one book a valuable tool for making factory improvements via process analysis.

Process analysis is not only one of the basic fields in IE, it is also a very important focus in QC, since QC uses process diagrams to analyze current conditions, identify improvement points, and plan standardization.

One of this book's main features is its emphasis on describing improvement steps. Improvements should be made according to the rules. Haste does indeed make waste, and QC demands a steady, methodical approach. This book also makes a point of backing up descriptions with specific case studies. After all, the book has been written for people who intend to put its lessons into practice in the factory. A third feature of the book is its additional focus on clerical process analysis aimed at improving service-related work.

Like QC techniques, IE techniques can be used by QC circles in their QC-related activities, and it is my hope that such small groups will find this book useful toward that end.

I am grateful to the many factories that provided the case studies for this book. I am also indebted to several authors whose publications served as invaluable references, particularly

---

* Productivity Press is publishing these four volumes as a set entitled *IE for the Shop Floor*; a translation of the *Motion Study* volume is available, and the other two volumes will follow in the future. — Ed.

the *Basic Course in IE for Managers* (authored by JUSE's Factory Industrial Engineering (FIE) council), and two double-volume works: *Factory IE* (by Katsuyoshi Ishihara) and *Work Site Improvement Methods* (by Messrs. Imaizumi, Konno, and Hara).

Finally, I would like to thank the JUSE publications staff for their generous assistance in producing this book.

Junichi Ishiwata

1

IE and Process Improvements

WHAT IS IE?

IE stands for industrial engineering. In a few words, IE is a group of techniques that can be used to eliminate waste, inconsistencies, and irrationalities from the workplace and provide high-quality goods and services easily, quickly, and inexpensively.

IE used to be something that managers and other upper-echelon staff designed and managed, but now all levels of factory and office workers are learning to use IE techniques as part of their improvement activities.

IE-related themes and IE techniques have been successfully used in many types of QC circle activities. You will see a few examples of this in Chapter 8 of this book. In these examples, workers use IE techniques to discover where waste, inconsistency, and irrationality (the "Big 3" problems) exist in their workplace, to make their work easier, and to produce better products or services more quickly and cheaply. As a result, they create a better work environment and contribute to the prosperity of the company as a whole.

IE may sound difficult, but it really is not. Like the seven QC tools, IE should be part of the improvement activities in any workplace.

IE techniques can be broken down generally into method improvement techniques and work measurement techniques; the following are commonly included:

Method improvement techniques

    1. Process analysis (this book's theme)
    2. Motion study
    3. Conveyance and equipment layout

Work measurement techniques

    4. Time study

Naturally, you should choose the IE techniques that suit the kinds of improvements to be made. Although these techniques can be used by themselves, they are closely interrelated and tend to reinforce each other when used in combination. An understanding of time study is especially helpful, since most IE measurements are time-based measurements.

For further description of motion study, conveyance and equipment layout, and time study, please refer to the corresponding volumes in this series. For our present purpose, it will suffice to briefly describe the main features of each of these IE techniques to help you know which techniques apply to which type of situation.

Method Improvement Techniques

Method improvement techniques help you understand and analyze the flow of operations so that you can discover where waste, inconsistency, and irrationality exist in those operations. Once you have discovered that, you have much less ground to cover in making improvements. At this stage, your most valuable tool for studying the overall flow of operations is process analysis. Motion study is the IE tool to use when you are studying, for example, how workers use their bodies when they operate switches. In addition, work processes often include conveyance stages or equipment layout schemes that may be efficient or not so efficient. Process analysis can help us evaluate their efficiency, but other IE techniques aimed specifically at conveyance and equipment layout can prove to be even more useful for improving those systems.

Work Measurement Techniques

Work measurement techniques can be used to measure time values within operations and to find out how much time each operation requires. Various time study methods have been developed — methods, in fact, too numerous to describe within the scope of this book. (For descriptions of the various time study methods, see the fourth volume in this series.)

To use the work measurement techniques, you must have time values for the various operations to be studied. Operation planning also requires such time measurements. However, operation time values have no meaning unless they lead to improvements that become firmly established as standard work procedures. Consequently, method improvement techniques and operation measurement techniques are mutually supportive and cannot be completely separated from one another.

MAKING IMPROVEMENTS BY THE RULES

You cannot hope for much success if you improvise your approach toward making improvements. There are two basic rules:

1. Follow the improvement steps.
2. Use the improvement methods.

IE is a hands-on activity. You learn IE by practicing it. After making several improvements, you will find that the rules are etched permanently in your consciousness. This knowledge can be gained only through practice; a merely theoretical grasp of them is of little value in making improvements.

Chapter 2 of this book focuses on the first rule. Following the improvement steps will enable you to avoid running hastily and ineffectively, like the hare who lost the race to the slow-but-steady tortoise.

The second rule is to use IE improvement methods. These include the seven QC tools (cause-and-effect diagrams, Pareto diagrams, check sheets, histograms, scatter diagrams, graphs and management charts, and stratification) as well as IE techniques. Another improvement method is function analysis, which sometimes falls under the category of value engineering.

The most important thing in making improvements is to start by obtaining an accurate understanding of the facts, such as the current conditions in the workplace. You must carefully analyze the current conditions to find out just where the problems lie. Sometimes this is a slow, painstaking process, but it is a crucial part of making improvements the right way: according to the rules.

As mentioned earlier, you cannot learn the rules by simply reading about them. Book study must be combined with hands-on practice, for it is through such practice that you will come to truly understand the rules. Accordingly, IE studies usually include lengthy practice sessions. The "Factory Industrial Engineering" (FIE) course that JUSE offers for factory managers includes a great deal of hands-on practice.

EVERY FACTORY IS A MOUNTAIN OF GOLD

Like a mountain full of undiscovered gold, every factory is rich in potential improvements, waiting to be made. This is true even if every imaginable improvement has already been made, for in today's climate of rapid technological progress, standing still means falling behind. That is just one reason why there is always room for improvement. Improvement is limitless.

You must resist the temptation to look at minor improvements as trivial matters. Seek out and implement even the smallest improvement. A pinch of dirt here and a pebble there can eventually add up to a mountain.

You also need to consider not only the improvements that will make your own workplace better but also those that will produce positive effects downstream. This is the "next process is our customer" philosophy. You will find increasing importance in this concept of providing the best possible service to the next stage of production. In fact, one of the main points of process improvements is to more closely link upstream and downstream processes for the sake of the production system as a whole.

Successful companies are made up of people who want improvement and are guided by a company policy that emphasizes the need for improvement. In manufacturing companies, process analysis is perhaps the most fundamental method in carrying out the endless and limitless process of making improvements.

2

Process Improvement Steps

This chapter describes the rules and steps to be followed in making process improvements. Readers familiar with the steps in the "QC stories" carried out by QC circles will recognize a close similarity between those steps and the process improvement steps described here. They differ mainly in where the lines are drawn between the steps. They are exactly alike in their liberal use of the PDCA improvement cycle (also described below).

Please refer to Figure 2-1 as you read the following description of the process improvement steps. These steps will guide you toward the most efficient way of making improvements and help you avoid shortsighted forays into apparent shortcuts that end up as long detours.

If you rush headlong toward making whatever improvement comes to mind, your improvement measure will probably not be very effective. Instead, you must begin by gaining a thorough grasp of the current situation. Once you understand exactly what the current conditions are, you are ready to begin looking for ways to improve them.

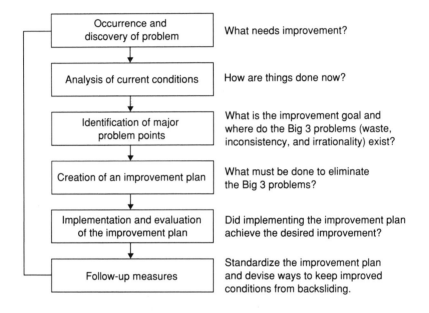

Occurrence and discovery of problem	What needs improvement?
Analysis of current conditions	How are things done now?
Identification of major problem points	What is the improvement goal and where do the Big 3 problems (waste, inconsistency, and irrationality) exist?
Creation of an improvement plan	What must be done to eliminate the Big 3 problems?
Implementation and evaluation of the improvement plan	Did implementing the improvement plan achieve the desired improvement?
Follow-up measures	Standardize the improvement plan and devise ways to keep improved conditions from backsliding.

Improvements are infinite. Therefore, the final step is to go back and find something else in need of improvement.

Figure 2-1. Process Improvement Steps

OCCURRENCE AND DISCOVERY OF PROBLEMS

Problems are not always easy to recognize. Consequently, you need to find ways to become more problem-conscious for the sake of improving the workplace. One way is to form QC circles whose activities include selecting problem-related themes and taking positive steps toward solving the problems.

Generally, you learn of problems either by discovering them yourself or by hearing about them from your boss or from a third party. Naturally, it is better to discover the problems yourself before someone else has to bring them to your attention. Likewise, it is better to solve problems in the making, as through QC activities, before they become real problems.

In addition to being generally aware of the problem points in your workplace, you should also maintain a solid grasp of the various statistical indicators of past conditions (in terms of efficiency, capacity utilization, yield, unit costs, and so on). It is also a good idea to keep informed of general conditions at other workshops in your factory and in factories of other companies, to know how your own workplace compares with others.

Problems rarely fit neatly into theme categories. Usually, their form is rather vague. Therefore, before you begin to ask yourself what the problem is and what improvement is needed to correct it, you should carry out a preliminary study using data from past improvement projects and from oral inquiries. Such a preliminary study may provide important background information that will help you recognize the problem and consolidate views about how it should be resolved.

Table 2-1 shows a PQCDSM (productivity, quality, cost, delivery, safety, morale) checklist, which is a helpful tool for identifying problems.

Table 2-1. PQCDSM Checklist

Item	Checkpoints
Productivity (P)	Has the production output been lower lately? Can it be raised? Has worker productivity been up to par?
Quality (Q)	Has quality been declining? Has the defect rate risen? Can the yield be raised? Has there been an increase in customer complaints?
Cost (C)	Have costs gone up? Have the unit costs of materials and fuels risen?
Delivery (D)	Have late deliveries increased? Can the production lead time be shortened?
Safety (S)	Have there been any safety problems? Has the number of accidents increased? Are people engaging in unsafe work practices?
Morale (M)	Is morale up or down? Are there any interpersonal problems? Are people getting appropriate job assignments?

Every workplace has its own assortment of problems; often many of the problems are interrelated. For example, improving the quality of just one product can make all the difference between timely and late delivery, and sometimes correcting one problem results in the correction of others. In such cases, the key is to find out what the most basic problem is. When there are several basic problems, you need to establish a priority list and solve them one at a time beginning with the most serious problem.

ANALYZING CURRENT CONDITIONS

Once you know that certain problems exist, you should establish a study plan and begin analyzing current conditions. Because the process analysis steps will be described in subsequent chapters, here we will look just briefly at the basic approach to analyzing current conditions.

Analyze the facts as they are

By using the 5W1H checklist shown in Table 2-2, you can be sure not to omit anything as you study the current conditions. When doing this, try to remain objective and view the facts as they are. Seeing the current conditions with your own eyes rather than relying on someone else's report is essential for maintaining objectivity.

Table 2-2. 5W1H Checklist

Item	5W1H Question	
Target	What	
Operator	Who	
Purpose	Why	Have these questions been asked?
Place or position	Where	
Time or period	When	
Method	How	

Use quantitative data to describe problem points

When describing problem points, try to get quantitative, measurable data and avoid vague qualitative descriptions. For example, you might use the following types of quantitative expressions to describe various factors that relate to the problem at hand:

Production output: tons per hour, units per hour, tons per day, kilograms per day, or lots per day

Lot size: tons per lot or units per lot

Required time: hours per lot or minutes per event

Required labor: people per lot, people per shift, or people per group

Transport distance: meters per trip, trips per hour, units per trip, and hours per trip

Use symbols and graphs to describe problems

Using symbols and graphs to describe problems makes the problem easier for other people to understand and analyze. Process analysis uses the process chart symbols described in Chapter 3. These symbols help distinguish among various steps in the process and make improvement points easier to recognize.

IDENTIFYING MAJOR PROBLEM POINTS

After analyzing the current conditions, you should be able to tell where the "Big 3" problems* exist within the operation processes and how bad the current conditions really are. This should enable you to identify the major problem points and establish improvement goals focused on those main points.

The process analysis steps described in the following chapters help you narrow your focus to the major problem points. You may find, for instance, that there are too many transportation trips, the transport distance is too long, or the conveyor is idle for too long.

At this point, you should gather up the results of your current condition analysis and meet with all concerned parties for a brainstorming session in which you draw up cause-and-effect diagrams and obtain input of ideas and opinions from everyone involved.

DRAFTING AN IMPROVEMENT PLAN

Once you know what the main problem points are and have established corresponding improvement goals, think about how you will achieve those goals. You may know where the Big 3 problems lie, but you still do not know how to eliminate them.

Naturally, since your workplace is the creation of your predecessors on the job, it may not be easy to make improvements. Nevertheless, you must look at the way in which everything is

---

* The Big 3 (sometimes called the "three *mus*" after their Japanese names — *muda, mura,* and *muri*) is a shorthand reference used in many Japanese factories to refer to waste, irrationality, and inconsistency. For more on the Big 3, see Tomo Sugiyama, *The Improvement Book* (Productivity Press, 1989) and Japan Human Relations Association (ed.), *The Idea Book* (Productivity Press, 1988) — Ed.

done in the workplace and ask yourself why must it be done that way and what would happen if you stopped doing it that way.

When doing this, remember the four basic principles for making process improvements:

1. Eliminate processes whenever possible
2. Simplify them
3. Combine them
4. Change the sequence

These rules should guide your thoughts as you draft your improvement plan (see Table 2-3).* You should also remember the fourfold purpose of making improvements: to make work easier (less fatiguing), to improve products or services (higher quality), to work faster (shorter lead times), and to produce goods or services less expensively (lower costs).

Table 2-3. Four Basic Principles for Making Improvements

Rule	Questions	Examples
Eliminate	Can this be eliminated? What will happen if we eliminate it?	• Eliminate or shorten inspection • Eliminate or shorten transportation by changing layout
Simplify	Can this be made simpler?	• Review operations • Automate
Combine	Can two or more processes be consolidated into one?	• Do two operations at the same time • Combine an operation with inspection
Change sequence	Can this operation be switched with another one?	• Increase efficiency by doing a later operation earlier

---

* For an extended discussion of these principles, see Ralph M. Barnes, *Motion and Time Study/Design and Measurement of Work*, 7th ed., (New York: John Wiley & Sons, 1980), p. 50 and following. — Ed.

Your improvement plan will probably have three stages of development:

First draft: Initial plan drafted without much revision
Second draft: Reworking of the initial draft based on various minor considerations
Final draft: Reworking of the second draft based on various major considerations

Depending on the circumstances, you may wish to select an improvement plan before it reaches the third stage. In any case, you need to get input and approval from your supervisors and other concerned parties before carrying out the plan.

IMPLEMENTING AND EVALUATING THE IMPROVEMENT PLAN

Once you have selected an improvement plan, you need to give it a trial run. Naturally, if the plan calls for major undertakings such as changing the equipment layout, a trial run is impossible. However, even if the plan calls for equipment modifications or layout changes, the data you have gathered during the initial study stage should enable you to estimate how the plan will affect factory operations and whether the plan is really feasible. The word *simulation* is used to describe this kind of data-based estimation.

Another part of the improvement plan's trial run is the training that will be needed to get workers used to the new way of doing things. If you neglect the need for training, your trial run will be less likely to produce good results.

New operational methods are rarely perfect right from the drawing board. You should expect to make various minor revisions to get the methods working right.

FOLLOW-UP MEASURES

If your evaluation of the improvement plan's trial run shows good results, you are ready to fully implement the plan. Such full implementation should include standardization and other tactics for ensuring that conditions do not revert to their former state.

Once you have completed your improvement and its follow-up work, you can begin looking for other improvement themes. Remember, progress rushes by those who stand still; there is always room for improvement.

3

Process Analysis

WHAT IS PROCESS ANALYSIS?

In a factory, various materials go through different processes and end up shipped out as products. This transformation from raw materials to finished products includes the steps, or stages, of operation, transportation, and inspection. Sometimes it also includes short- or long-term delays.

The method for describing and analyzing these various steps in a process is called process analysis. Process analysis can be summed up as the description and analysis of the entire series of manufacturing steps, with a view toward finding and eliminating the Big 3 problems (waste, irrationality, and inconsistency) in and between these steps by identifying improvement needs and devising ways to meet those needs.

As such, process analysis looks at the overall flow of work to find ways of improving this flow. Process analysis is the foundation of method improvement techniques. Although it is sometimes all you will need to complete an improvement, many situations will also require other methods, such as motion study or improvement of conveyance and equipment layout. Process analysis is just one milestone on the way to improvement.

THE PURPOSE OF PROCESS ANALYSIS

Work that consists of the same operations performed day in and day out tends to be taken for granted as the best possible way of doing things. As a result, there is no progress or improvement.

To escape this trap, remember to continually look for things in need of improvement and to improve them. In process analysis, you do this by making the following considerations:

1. Study the flow of processes.
2. Find where waste exists in the flow of processes.
3. Consider whether the processes can be rearranged into a more efficient sequence.
4. Consider whether the flow of processes is smooth enough and whether there are any problems in the equipment layout or the transport system.
5. Consider whether everything being done at each process is really necessary and what would happen if superfluous tasks were removed.

Various IE techniques can be used to improve the way work is being done. While IE techniques such as time study, motion study, and conveyance and layout study are all useful for improving certain detailed aspects of the work being done, process analysis is always your primary tool for finding and eliminating the Big 3 from the various work processes.

Process analysis is the method that best ensures a thorough grasp of the processes and addresses not only the individual processes where problems exist but also the upstream and downstream processes that are related to the process in question. This helps you gain a deeper understanding of the problem and thereby makes it easier to recognize just what kind of improvement is needed to solve the problem.

TYPES OF PROCESS ANALYSIS

When the main object of analysis is the product, the analysis is called *product process analysis*; when the object is the operator, it is called *operator process analysis*.

If you are studying the operator and the equipment together or an operation that is jointly done by several operators, your analysis is called *joint process analysis* in general and either *operator-machine analysis* or *joint operation analysis* in particular.

As process analysis has been extended to clerical operations, the term *clerical process analysis* has recently come into use.

Thus, the specific analytical methods used in process analysis differ according to the object of your analysis. These various types of process analysis are outlined in Figure 3-1.

Although these different types of process analysis are basically similar, each has its own special characteristics. These characteristics will be described in Chapter 4.

PROCESS CHART SYMBOLS

Process chart symbols are the predetermined symbols used to describe the flow of processes as part of process analysis. In Japan, these symbols have been standardized under Japanese Industrial Standards JIS Z 8206. Use only standardized symbols whenever possible.*

---

* Another standardized version that may be used is ASME Standard 101, "Operation and Flow Process Charts," which uses an arrow for transport rather than the small circle, and has one symbol for both qualitative and quantitative inspections. See Ralph M. Barnes, *Motion and Time Study/Design and Measurement of Work*, 7th ed., (New York: John Wiley & Sons, 1980). — Ed.

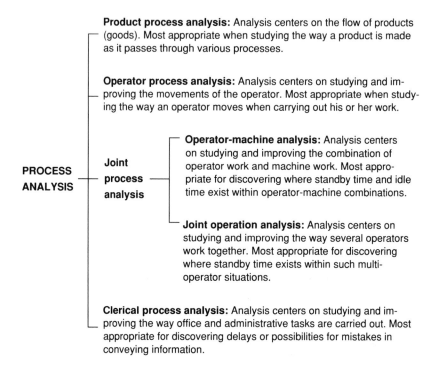

Product process analysis: Analysis centers on the flow of products (goods). Most appropriate when studying the way a product is made as it passes through various processes.

Operator process analysis: Analysis centers on studying and improving the movements of the operator. Most appropriate when studying the way an operator moves when carrying out his or her work.

PROCESS
ANALYSIS

Joint
process
analysis

Operator-machine analysis: Analysis centers on studying and improving the combination of operator work and machine work. Most appropriate for discovering where standby time and idle time exist within operator-machine combinations.

Joint operation analysis: Analysis centers on studying and improving the way several operators work together. Most appropriate for discovering where standby time exists within such multi-operator situations.

Clerical process analysis: Analysis centers on studying and improving the way office and administrative tasks are carried out. Most appropriate for discovering delays or possibilities for mistakes in conveying information.

Figure 3-1. Types of Process Analysis

Using standardized symbols makes it easier for other people to read your process charts. It also makes it easier to recognize where problems lie (such as too much standby time between processes or too many transportation trips), and this obviously makes it easier to identify improvement points.

Under JIS Z 8206, process chart symbols are broken down into basic and supplementary symbols. The basic chart symbols are used to describe basic steps such as those involving operations, transportation, storage, delay, volume inspection, and quality inspection. These symbols are described in Table 3-1.

Supplementary chart symbols are used to indicate the flow of processes. They include symbols indicating line of flow, divisions, and omissions. These symbols are described in Table 3-2.

Table 3-1. Basic Graphic Symbols (JIS Z 8206)

No.	Basic Step	Specific Step	Symbol	Meaning	Comment
1	Operation	Operation	◯	Alters the shape or other characteristics of a material, semi-finished product, or product	
2	Transportation	Transportation	◯ (⇨)	Changes the location of a material, semi-finished product, or product	The transportation symbol is a circle half the diameter of the circle used as the operation symbol. An arrow can be used in place of this small circle. The direction of the arrow does not imply the direction of transportation.
3	Retention	Storage	▽	A scheduled accumulation of materials, parts, or products	
4		Delay	D	An unscheduled accumulation of materials, parts, or products	
5	Inspection	Volume inspection	▢	Measurement of amounts of materials, parts, or products for comparison with the specified amounts to judge whether a discrepancy exists	
6		Quality inspection	◇	Testing and visual inspection of materials, parts, or products for comparison with quality standards to judge whether defective (substandard) products are being produced.	

Table 3-2. Supplementary Symbols (JIS Z 8206)

No.	Symbol Name	Symbol	Meaning	Comments
1	Line of flow			Describes the sequence of basic steps	If the sequential relationship of steps is hard to understand, use arrows at the middle or end of the line to indicate the process flow direction.
2	Division	⌇⌇⌇	Indicates division of responsibility for ease of diagramming	
3	Omission	═══	Indicates omission (abbreviation) of part of the process flow	

When one process includes two functions, you can use a combination of basic chart symbols to describe the two functions. Table 3-3 shows some examples of combined symbols.

Table 3-3. Examples of Basic Graphic Symbol Combinations

Symbol	Meaning
◇□	Step is mainly quality inspection, but includes some volume inspection
□◇	Step is mainly volume inspection, but includes some quality inspection
○□	Step is mainly operation, but includes some volume inspection
○◇	Step is mainly operation, but includes some quality inspection
○⇨	Step is mainly operation, but includes some transportation

The process chart symbols are the most widely used analytical tool in process analysis. When performing product process analysis, you will use them as just described. The symbols used for operator process analysis are almost the same as these, but the ones used for joint process analysis and clerical process analysis are quite different. These other symbols will be described in subsequent chapters.

4

Product Process Analysis

WHAT IS PRODUCT PROCESS ANALYSIS?

Product process analysis is an analytical method used to study the flow of operations in terms of the materials, parts, and/or products being handled at those processes. Product process analysis uses some of the same principal techniques of process analysis in general, so the techniques described in this chapter will apply within the framework of other process analysis techniques as well.

According to Japanese Industrial Standard JIS Z 8206, which describes graphic symbols used in process analysis charts, there are four types of product processes: linear, converging, branching, and compound. Generally, two or more of these types will be combined. When analyzing product processes, your first step should be to pay special attention to the branching and converging types of product processes and to understand the flow of products.

Linear Processes

When the sequence of steps that transform materials into products is all in one line, it is called a linear product process. In the example shown in Figure 4-1, material (steel) is rolled, then inspected, packaged, and held for shipment. The figure uses process chart symbols to show the flow of the material through the processes. This product process chart contains no convergence; it is simply one line of processes.

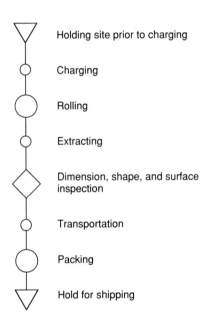

Holding site prior to charging

Charging

Rolling

Extracting

Dimension, shape, and surface inspection

Transportation

Packing

Hold for shipping

Figure 4-1. Linear Process (Example)

Converging Processes

The converging product process line usually consists of stages where parts, purchased goods, and other materials are assembled to make a product. In chemical factories, for example, where products are made from many ingredients, there may be dozens of process lines leading into the main line where the ingredients are combined.

In the example shown in Figure 4-2, a sub pipe line converges with a main pipe line, where the two types of pipe are welded together and checked under a certain amount of water pressure. This type of line configuration requires some care about the lot sizes being handled on the two converging lines.

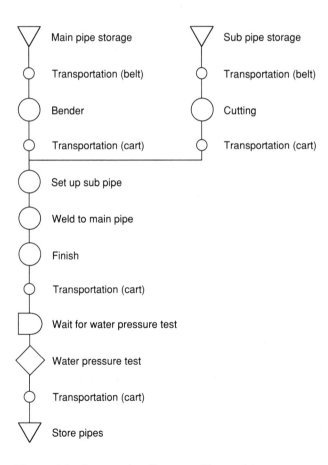

Figure 4-2. Converging Process (Example)

Branching Processes

The branching process line configuration is the reverse of the converging type in that a single line is split into two or more lines, as happens when chemical factories produce more than one type of product from a certain chemical ingredient. The branching type is also known as the diverging type.

In the example shown in Figure 4-3, iron ore is crushed and screened, and then the crushed ore is sent via one branch process line to a sintering plant while the lump ore is sent via another branch process line to a blast furnace. This type of configuration requires consideration of the lot sizes being carried to the branch process lines.

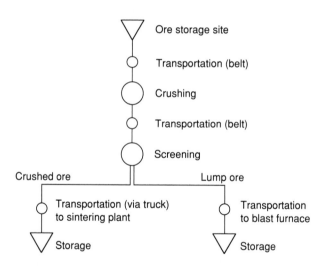

Figure 4-3. Branching Process (Example)

Compound Processes

This type includes process line configurations that branch out at one point and converge again at another point. There are two sorts of compound line configurations:

- Those in which a branch line returns to the main line at the same point where it left
- Those in which a branch line returns to the main line at a point downstream

Figure 4-4 shows an example of the first sort of compound line configuration. In this example, some steel material is about to be rolled, as in Figure 4-1, but a rework step occurs prior to subsequent rolling of the same steel material. After this material has been rolled a specified number of times, it is sent to the packing process and then held for shipping. This type of configuration is becoming rare due to greater use of continuous line configurations, but it still exists at some factories.

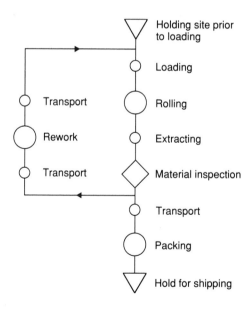

Figure 4-4. Compound Process (Example 1)

Figure 4-5 shows an example of the second sort of compound line configuration. In this example, the steel rolling process is followed by an inspection process. Only those inspected items that are judged to be in need of rework are sent via the branch process line to the rework process, after which they converge back onto the main process line to join the other items that were sent straight to the packing stage after inspection.

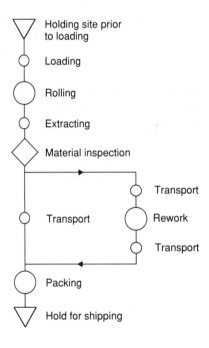

Figure 4-5. Compound Process (Example 2)

THE PURPOSE OF PRODUCT PROCESS ANALYSIS

Product process analysis is a technique for studying the flow of goods through a process line in order to redesign or otherwise improve the sequence of processing operations. The purpose of doing it is to find a way to make better products more easily, cheaply, and quickly.

To achieve this purpose, process charts (and the corresponding graphic symbols) are used to describe and study the sequence of work processes, in conjunction with top-view flow diagrams used to study what goes on within each operation. Using these tools together is a very effective way to find and eliminate the Big 3 problems from tasks at each process.

In keeping with the four basic principles of improvement described in Table 2-3, the purpose of product process analysis is to check for

- unnecessary delay points along the line,
- unnecessary transportation trips,
- unnecessarily long transportation distances,
- problems posed by the choice of transportation method, and
- opportunities to combine operations and inspection,

while studying ways to improve

- the equipment layout,
- the sequence of work, and
- the distribution of workloads.

If you look at each of these points, you have a good chance of discovering and establishing better work methods.

STEPS IN PRODUCT PROCESS ANALYSIS

Step 1: Conduct a Preliminary Study

As pointed out in Chapter 2, the first process improvement step is a preliminary study to clarify the problem points before making the actual product process analysis. It is much better to go to the factory and study the conditions firsthand than to rely on written or oral descriptions that others have made. This study should cover the following areas:

1. Production volume of product (planned and actual)
2. Description of product and relevant quality standards

    3. Inspection standards (for intermediate inspection, pre-shipment inspection, yield, etc.)

    4. Equipment layout

    5. Process flow (branching and converging process lines, etc.)

    6. Materials (types and units)

Step 2: Draw Up a Process Flow Chart

Refer to Tables 3-1, 3-2, and 3-3 (Chapter 3) as you draw up a process flow chart to describe the product's path through the process line.

When drawing this chart, carefully consider and distinguish among the main types of steps included in the process line: operations, transportation, inspection, and retention. Among retention steps, be sure to distinguish between storage (a scheduled accumulation of materials, parts, or products) and simple delay (an unscheduled accumulation of materials, parts, or products). Also break down inspection into volume inspection and quality inspection. These distinctions will be very important later in the analysis.

When looking at the actual flow of process steps, it is sometimes hard to tell just where an operation step ends and a retention step begins. Nevertheless, you need to make as clear a distinction as possible among these different steps, since you will be making time measurements of each operation later on in the analysis.

Step 3: Record Measurements for All Required Items in Each Process

Once you have drawn up a flow chart, you need to measure various items in each process and record the measurements. These measurements must be made firsthand at the factory.

You may want to use a preprinted process chart worksheet such as the one shown in Figure 4-6. Or it may be helpful to make a table with columns for the elements of the 5W1H formula. Table 4-1 shows an example of a completed measurement worksheet using 5W1H as a framework.

The 4M checklist (man/woman, machine, material, and method) is another set of items that can be used for a worksheet to check the required measurements. In the "machine" column, enter measurements of equipment, jigs, sites, and the like. In the "man/woman" column, enter the number of people required for each process; if it helps the analysis, you can enter the names of individual workers. Entering the time required for each process is a must. For transportation steps, be sure to measure and record both the transportation time and distance.

Product process analysis is easy enough when products flow one at a time through the line, but in many instances the products are operated on, transported, and inspected in batches. For the sake of analysis, consider each of these batches as a specific lot size that will serve as the basic quantitative unit in the analysis. Similarly, determine analytical units (of 10s, 100s, by weight, or whatever) for products that are made via a continuous manufacturing system.

To analyze transportation distances or time when a quantitative unit is processed several times, use the following formula:

Transportation distance = distance per trip × no. of trips

Example: 10m × 5 trips = 50m

Transportation time = time of one trip × no. of trips

Example: 3 min. × 5 trips = 15 min.

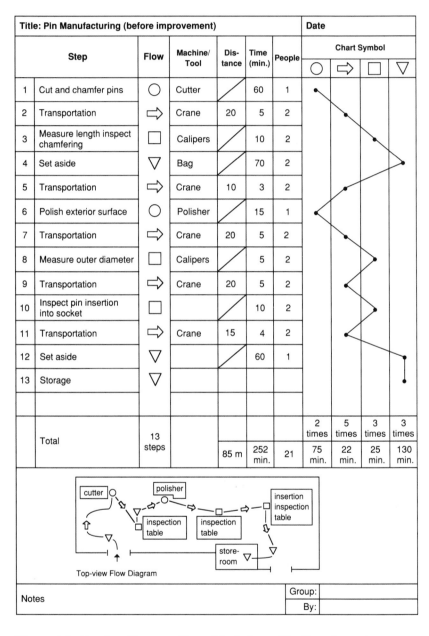

Title: Pin Manufacturing (before improvement)						Date				
Step	**Flow**	**Machine/ Tool**	**Dis- tance**	**Time (min.)**	**People**	**Chart Symbol**				
						○	⇨	□	▽	
1	Cut and chamfer pins	○	Cutter		60	1				
2	Transportation	⇨	Crane	20	5	2				
3	Measure length inspect chamfering	□	Calipers		10	2				
4	Set aside	▽	Bag		70	2				
5	Transportation	⇨	Crane	10	3	2				
6	Polish exterior surface	○	Polisher		15	1				
7	Transportation	⇨	Crane	20	5	2				
8	Measure outer diameter	□	Calipers		5	2				
9	Transportation	⇨	Crane	20	5	2				
10	Inspect pin insertion into socket	□			10	2				
11	Transportation	⇨	Crane	15	4	2				
12	Set aside	▽			60	1				
13	Storage	▽								
Total		13 steps		85 m	252 min.	21	2 times 75 min.	5 times 22 min.	3 times 25 min.	3 times 130 min.

Top-view Flow Diagram

Notes		Group:
		By:

Figure 4-6. Product Process Chart Worksheet: Pin Manufacturing Case Study

Table 4-1. 5W1H Worksheet for Product Process Analysis

Step	Activity (and Why?)	Personnel (Who?)	Machine/Equipment (What?)	Location (Where?)	Time (When?)	Method (How?)
Operation	(specific description of operation)	(job name, no. of workers, worker names, etc.)	(machine name, equipment name, jig name, no. of units, etc.)	(specific description of processing site)	(processing time, production output (per-unit time), etc.)	(specific description of processing sequence)
Transportation	(specific description of transportation task)	(same as above)	(name of equipment involved)	(from where to where and distance)	(transportation time)	(units per transportation trip, loading and unloading methods, etc.)
Inspection	(specific description of inspection items)	(same as above)	(inspection equipment, inspection tools, etc.)	(inspection site)	(inspection time)	(inspection methods, pass/fail criteria, defect treatment measures, etc.)
Retention	(clear description of retention status (delay, storage, held for shipment, etc.))	(storage staff, etc.)	(storage site, storage equipment, etc.)	(storage site)	(retention time)	(method of storage (containers, etc.))

Figure 4-6 also shows a flow diagram drawn on the bottom part of the process chart form. This kind of layout diagram shows at a glance how the products flow in the factory as various goods move through various operations.

Step 4: Organize the Analysis Results

After recording the measurements on a process chart form, organize the data as shown in Table 4-2. In this table, only the operation steps add value to the product — the transportation, inspection, and retention steps add no value. Consequently, it is best to minimize these latter operations; your next objective is to find ways to do that. Even in the operations themselves, look for ways to shorten processing time and to make it easier and simpler (requiring fewer labor-hours).

Table 4-2. Process Analysis Data Chart

	No. of Steps	Time (min.)	Distance (m)	Staff (people)
Operation ○	2	75	—	2
Transportation ⇨	5	22	85	10
Inspection ☐	3	25	—	6
Retention ▽	3	(130)	—	3
Total	13	122	85	21

Step 5: Draft an Improvement Plan

Using the product process chart worksheet and flow diagram (Figure 4-6), along with your organized data (Table 4-2), you are now ready to pick out the problem points and start devising improvements to solve the problems.

At this point, it is very important to solicit input from all concerned parties. As in QC circle activities, when more minds are brought together to ponder a problem, more improvement ideas are generated. It may also be helpful to sort everyone's improvement concerns by process steps, as shown in Table 4-3.

Table 4-3. Improvement Concerns

Step	Improvement Concern
Overall	1. Where are the major improvement points in terms of • the overall factors such as total time, total transportation distance, and total required labor-hours • the operation-specific values for each of those factors? (Use Pareto charts if needed to elucidate these improvement points.) 2. Can any of the operations be eliminated? 3. Can any of the operations be done simultaneously with another one? 4. Can the sequence of operations be changed to reduce the number of operations, required time, transportation distance, or number of workers?
Operations ○	1. Do any of the operations have an extra-long processing time? If so, check whether other IE methods (such as motion or time study) can be used to improve the processing method. 2. Can the equipment's performance be improved? 3. Can two operations be combined at one site? 4. Can improvements be made by changing the sequence of operations? 5. Is the current production lot size too large or too small?
Transportation ⇨	1. Can the number of trips be reduced? 2. Can necessary transportation be done simultaneously with operations (such as by processing materials as they are being conveyed on carts, etc.)? 3. Can the transportation time be shortened? 4. Can the layout be changed to eliminate part of the transportation?

Table 4-3. (cont.)

Step	Improvement Concern
Transportation ⇨ (continued)	5. Can the operation and inspection sites be combined to eliminate the need for transportation between them? 6. Can the lot size per trip be increased to reduce the number of trips? 7. Do loading and unloading take up a lot of time? 8. Can the transportation equipment be improved? 9. Can the sling jigs be improved?
Inspection ◇,□	1. Can the number of inspections be reduced? 2. Are any inspections unnecessary and expendable? 3. Can necessary inspections be done while the product is being processed? In other words, can the circle and diamond symbols be combined (as either **diamond in circle** or **square in circle**) to reduce labor-hours or total time and/or eliminate transportation? 4. Are quality inspections and volume inspections being done at separate processes? Can the two be combined at the same process? 5. Can the inspection methods be improved (such as sped up)?
Retention ▽,D	1. Can the number of delays be reduced? 2. Can operation and inspection sites be combined to eliminate temporary storage? Especially in cases where retention before and after an operation is not balanced, can operations be combined to remove the delay caused by the imbalance? 3. Can retention times be shortened?

Draft your improvement plans based on a consideration of improvement ideas such as those listed in Table 4-3. It's a good idea to prepare at least two or three plans so that you can compare them and get input about them from supervisors or other interested parties.

The next step is to draw flow diagrams and process flow charts that illustrate your improvement plans. Using the example shown in Figure 4-6, assume that you are going to improve the layout and thereby reduce the number of delay points and transportation trips; perhaps you will combine the outer dimension measurement process with the insertion inspection process to save labor-hours, total time, and transportation distance. Figure 4-7 shows the results of such an improvement as they would appear on a product process chart for the planned improvement.

If possible, also try to adjust the layout shown in the flow chart (Figure 4-7) and measure the result. Ordinarily, moving equipment around costs time and money, so it's good to estimate beforehand how much improvement such a rearrangement would bring in terms of time, distances, and labor-hours. To do this, organize your data into a product process chart (Figure 4-7) and data chart (Table 4-4) based on the improvement plan. Next, compare the two sets of data, before improvement and based on the improvement plan (see Table 4-5).

Table 4-4. Data Chart (Improvement Plan)

	No. of Steps	Time (min.)	Distance (m)	People
Operation ◯	2	75	—	2
Transportation ⇨	4	17	65	8
Inspection ☐	2	25	—	4
Retention ▽	1	(0)	—	0
Total	9	117	65	14

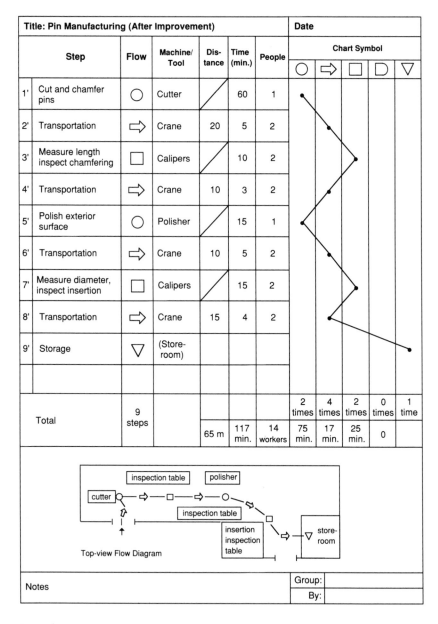

Title: Pin Manufacturing (After Improvement)						Date					
Step	**Flow**	**Machine/Tool**	**Distance**	**Time (min.)**	**People**	**Chart Symbol**					
						○	⇨	□	D	▽	
1' Cut and chamfer pins	○	Cutter		60	1						
2' Transportation	⇨	Crane	20	5	2						
3' Measure length inspect chamfering	□	Calipers		10	2						
4' Transportation	⇨	Crane	10	3	2						
5' Polish exterior surface	○	Polisher		15	1						
6' Transportation	⇨	Crane	10	5	2						
7' Measure diameter, inspect insertion	□	Calipers		15	2						
8' Transportation	⇨	Crane	15	4	2						
9' Storage	▽	(Storeroom)									
Total	9 steps					2 times	4 times	2 times	0 times	1 time	
			65 m	117 min.	14 workers	75 min.	17 min.	25 min.	0		

Top-view Flow Diagram

Notes	Group:
	By:

Figure 4-7. Product Process Chart (After Improvement)

Table 4-5. Comparison of Current Conditions with Planned Improvement

Step	No. of Steps			Time (min.)			Distance (m)			People		
	Before Improvement	Improvement Plan	Effect	Before Improvement	Improvement Plan	Effect	Before Improvement	Improvement Plan	Effect	Before Improvement	Improvement Plan	Effect
Oper-ation	2	2	0	75	75	0	—	—	—	2	2	0
Trans-portation	5	4	1	22	17	5	85	65	20	10	8	2
Inspec-tion	3	2	1	25	25	0	—	—	—	6	4	2
Reten-tion	3	1	2	(130)	(0)	(130)	—	—	—	3	0	3
Total	13	9	4	122	117	5	85	65	20	21	14	7

Step 6: Implement and Evaluate the Improvement Plan

Once your improvement plan has been approved, you can implement it. When doing this, be sure to provide adequate training to make up for inexperience with any new work methods. Measure and evaluate the improvement results only after the workers have become proficient in the new work methods. Any abnormalities that appear during implementation should be addressed affirmatively and promptly.

Step 7: Standardize the Improvement Plan

If the evaluation shows that the improvement plan has produced the predicted results, do not hesitate to standardize the improvement to prevent backsliding. Remember, no improvement plan is perfect, and there is always room for further improvement via follow-up measures. Improvement is limitless.

EXAMPLES OF PRODUCT PROCESS ANALYSIS

The following case studies of product process analysis were selected from fieldwork reports submitted by students in JUSE's FIE seminar, a basic IE course for supervisors and managers.

The first case study's theme is a processing sequence improvement that reduced the number of steps in the line and also shortened the manufacturing time, lowered personnel requirements, moved up the delivery date, and cut costs. The focus of the second case study is an improvement of the factory layout, which resulted in a better flow of operations, less delay time, and a shorter production lead time. The third case study features an improvement plan that called for a change in the processing jigs to combine three operations, which not only reduced the number of steps but also shortened the processing time.

All three case studies describe typical improvements that can be made in most factories; none of them were particularly difficult to carry out. Reading these case studies may help you to recognize how your own factory can be improved.

CASE STUDY 1

**Machining Parts for Rotary Drive Mechanisms in Helicopters
Report by: Katsuhiro Nagashima, Nippon Hikoki KK (Japan
Aircraft Co., Ltd.), Sugita Plant**

Reason for Making Improvement

Our customers for these parts demand three things of us: quality, prompt delivery, and low cost. We had no problem with the quality requirement, but we had trouble keeping our delivery schedule and costs within the desired ranges. We got complaints from customers about each shipment, and they were beginning to lose confidence in our company.

In an effort to find out where the Big 3 problems existed in our manufacturing processes, we carried out product process analysis and consequently were able to make some improvements.

Outline of Processes

Figure 4-8 shows an outline of these processes. Figure 4-9 shows what the part looks like before and after this sequence.

Product Process Analysis

Step 1: Conduct a preliminary study

In our preliminary study, we found, among other things, that the machining line included a total of 19 steps, from surface-finishing the bottom surface to storing the machined part.

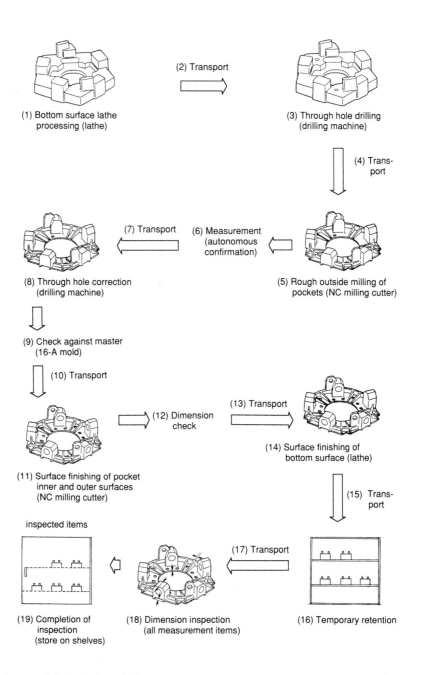

Figure 4-8. Outline of Steps

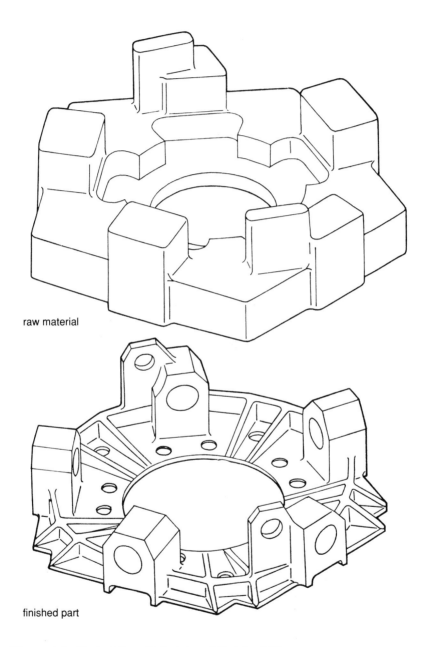

raw material

finished part

Figure 4-9. Part at Raw Material and Finished Stages

Step 2: Draw up a process flow chart

Our flow chart is included in the product process chart shown in Figure 4-10.

Step 3: Record measurements for all required items in each process

Figure 4-10 also includes a listing of the machines and jigs used at each process, the required processing time, and staff requirements that we measured during our product process analysis. Part (a) of Figure 4-11 shows a layout chart (before improvement) that we submitted as our flow diagram.

Step 4: Organize the analysis results

Table 4-6 shows how we organized our analysis results.

Step 5: Draft an improvement plan

As the data chart in Table 4-6 and the pre-improvement layout chart in Figure 4-11 (a) show, the product must make several trips between the drilling machine and the NC milling cutter. This stood out as an area that could stand improvement.

We looked for ways to bring together all of the drilling machine processes and the NC milling cutter processes and found that it was technically feasible to do that. Figure 4-12 shows the product process chart that we drew up when working out this improvement, and Figure 4-11 (b) shows the layout specified in our improvement plan. Table 4-7 compares the various process measurements before improvement with the improvement plan. Figure 4-13 shows a path diagram of the process sequence before improvement and as specified in the improvement plan.

Title: Part for Rotary Drive Mechanism						Date			
Step	Flow	Machine/ Tool	Dis-tance	Time (min.)	People	○	⇨	□	▽
1 Lathe bottom surface	○	Lathe		45	1				
2 Transportation	⇨	Cart	15	1	1				
3 Drill through holes (reference holes)	○	Drilling machine		20	1				
4 Transportation	⇨	Cart	10	1	1				
5 Mill pockets and shave down perimeter	○	NC milling cutter		180	1				
6 Measure (autonomous confirmation)	□	Calipers		5	1				
7 Transportation	⇨	Cart	10	1	1				
8 Correct through holes	○	Drilling machine		15	1				
9 Check against master mold	□	16A mold		1	1				
10 Transportation	⇨	Cart	10	1	1				
11 Mill pockets and finish perimeter surfaces	○	NC milling cutter		150	1				
12 Dimension check	□	Calipers, micrometer		5	1				
13 Transportation	⇨	Cart	5	1	1				
14 Surface finishing of bottom surface (lathe)	○	Lathe		30	1				
15 Transportation	⇨	Cart	30	2	1				
16 Temporary holding	▽			30					
17 Transportation	⇨	Hand carry	2	0.5	1				
18 Dimension inspection	□	Calipers, micrometer		15	1				
19 Storage	▽	Storage shelf							
Total	19 steps		82 m	503.5 min.	17 people	6 times (440 min.)	7 times (7.5 min.)	4 times (26 min.)	2 times (30 min.)

Notes:
1. Special carrier boxes are used to convey the parts, since each part weighs 15 kilograms.
2. The operations correspond to the numbers in the process outline shown in Figure 4-8.

Figure 4-10. Product Process Chart (Before Improvement)

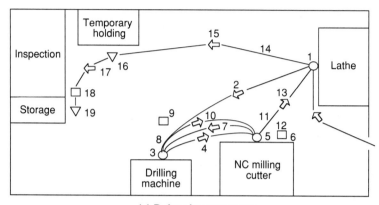

(a) Before Improvement

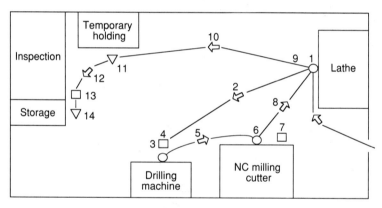

(b) After Improvement

Figure 4-11. Flow Diagrams (Before Improvement and According to Improvement Plan)

Table 4-6. Data Chart (Before Improvement)

	No. of Steps	Time (min.)	Distance (m)	Staff (people)
Operation ○	6	440	—	6
Transportation ⇨	7	7.5	82	7
Inspection ☐	4	26	—	4
Retention ▽	2	30	—	—
Total	19	503.5	82	25

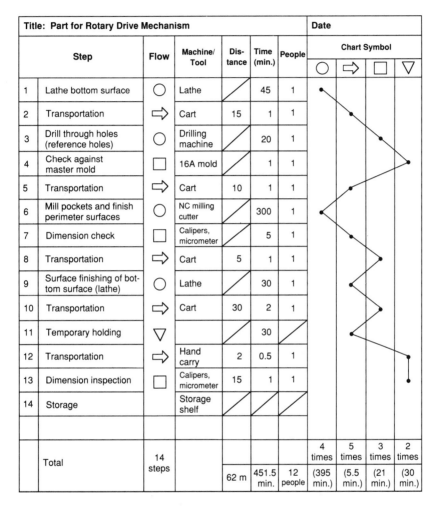

Title: Part for Rotary Drive Mechanism						Date			
Step	Flow	Machine/ Tool	Dis- tance	Time (min.)	People	Chart Symbol			
						○	⇨	☐	▽
1	Lathe bottom surface	○	Lathe		45	1			
2	Transportation	⇨	Cart	15	1	1			
3	Drill through holes (reference holes)	○	Drilling machine		20	1			
4	Check against master mold	☐	16A mold		1	1			
5	Transportation	⇨	Cart	10	1	1			
6	Mill pockets and finish perimeter surfaces	○	NC milling cutter		300	1			
7	Dimension check	☐	Calipers, micrometer		5	1			
8	Transportation	⇨	Cart	5	1	1			
9	Surface finishing of bottom surface (lathe)	○	Lathe		30	1			
10	Transportation	⇨	Cart	30	2	1			
11	Temporary holding	▽			30				
12	Transportation	⇨	Hand carry	2	0.5	1			
13	Dimension inspection	☐	Calipers, micrometer	15	1	1			
14	Storage		Storage shelf						
Total		14 steps		62 m	451.5 min.	12 people	4 times (395 min.)	5 times (5.5 min.)	3 times (21 min.)	2 times (30 min.)

Figure 4-12.   Product Process Chart (Improvement Plan)

Step 6: Implement and evaluate the improvement plan

To find out what kind of quality changes might result from the improvement plan, we conducted a trial production run. We were afraid that a warping problem might develop, since warping was a constant threat even before the improvement.

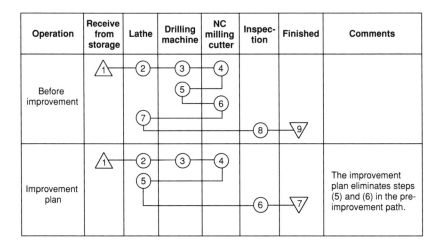

Figure 4-13. Path Diagram (Before Improvement and According to Improvement Plan)

Table 4-7. Comparison of Current Conditions with Planned Improvement

Step		Before Improvement	Improvement Plan	Net Reduction
Operations	No. of times	6	4	2
	Time (min.)	440	395	45
	Distance (m)	—	—	—
	People	6	4	2
Trans-portation	No. of times	7	5	2
	Time (min.)	7.5	5.5	2
	Distance (m)	82	62	20
	People	7	5	2
Inspection	No. of times	4	3	1
	Time (min.)	26	21	5
	Distance (m)	—	—	—
	People	4	3	1
Retention	No. of times	2	2	0
	Time (min.)	30	30	0
	Distance (m)	—	—	—
	People	—	—	—
Total	No. of times	19	14	5
	Time (min.)	503.5	451.5	52
	Distance (m)	82	62	20
	People	17	12	5

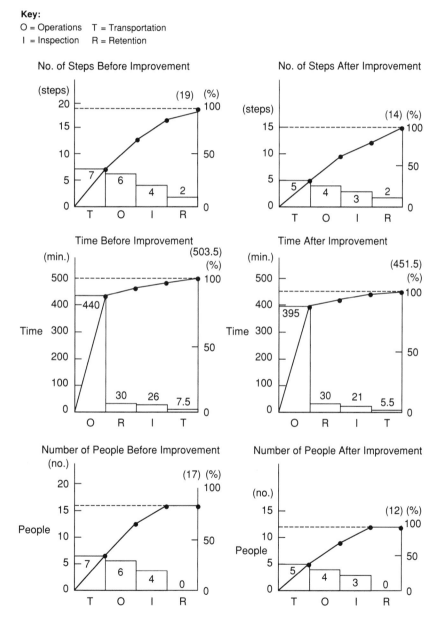

**Figure 4-14. Pareto Charts Comparing Pre-improvement and
                  Post-improvement Measurements**

Fortunately, almost no warping happened during our trial run. Satisfied with the quality results, we decided to go ahead with full implementation of the improvement plan.

Figure 4-14 shows the Pareto charts that we drew up to compare the improvement results with pre-improvement measurements in terms of the number of processes, manufacturing time, and labor requirements. As these charts show, we achieved all the improvements targeted by the plan.

Step 7: Standardize the improvement plan

We changed our line operations as specified by the improvement plan and retrained all our workers in the new procedures.

Conclusion

Thanks to this successful improvement, we no longer receive complaints from customers regarding our delivery schedule and production costs. We can now expect our customers to have the utmost confidence in our work. We also expect that this improvement will result in higher profits for our company.

CASE STUDY 2

Eliminating the Big 3 Problems from Product Assembly Operations
Report by: Keizo Komiyama, Yazaki Buhin KK (Yazaki Parts Co., Ltd.), Gotemba Plant

---

Goal

Our group carried out product process analysis to discover where the Big 3 problems (waste, inconsistency, and irrationality) exist in our product assembly operations. Our goal was to shorten production lead time and improve the flow of operations by eliminating these adverse factors.

Outline of Processes

Our company, an automotive parts manufacturer, makes bundled wire parts for connecting various electrical parts and electric motor-driven parts that are used in automobiles. Figure 4-15 shows the processes that lead to our finished product. The processes being targeted by the improvement theme described in this report are shown as processes *D* through *H*.

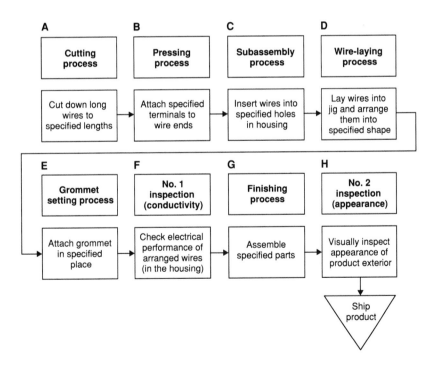

Figure 4-15. Outline of Steps

Product Process Analysis

Step 1: Conduct a preliminary study

Our preliminary study of the process flow showed that the flow converged and that there were many delay sites in the operations. To improve the flow, we needed to reduce the number of these delay sites, so we carried out our product process analysis with this objective in mind.

Step 2: Draw up a process flow chart

The product process chart in Figure 4-16 includes our process flow chart. There are 21 steps altogether, from subassembly transportation to warehouse storage.

Step 3: Record measurements for all required items in each process

Figure 4-16 also includes a listing of the machines and jigs used for each operation, the transportation distances, required processing time, and personnel requirements that we measured during our product process analysis. Figure 4-17 shows a layout chart (before improvement) that we submitted as our flow diagram.

Step 4: Organize the analysis results

Table 4-8 shows how we organized our analysis results.

Step 5: Draft an improvement plan

Armed with our product process chart and layout diagram, we held a brainstorming session with all concerned parties and came up with the following two-part improvement plan.

1. Since the wire-laying process takes the longest and since the operations at the processes that follow grommet

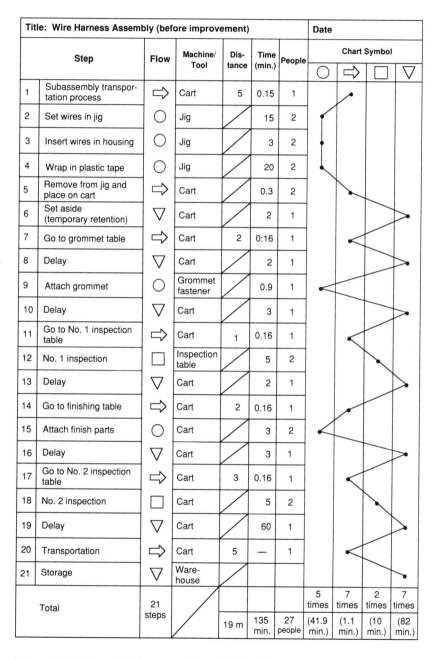

	Step	Flow	Machine/Tool	Distance	Time (min.)	People	Chart Symbol ◯	⇨	☐	▽
	Title: Wire Harness Assembly (before improvement)						**Date**			
1	Subassembly transportation process	⇨	Cart	5	0.15	1				
2	Set wires in jig	◯	Jig		15	2				
3	Insert wires in housing	◯	Jig		3	2				
4	Wrap in plastic tape	◯	Jig		20	2				
5	Remove from jig and place on cart	⇨	Cart		0.3	2				
6	Set aside (temporary retention)	▽	Cart		2	1				
7	Go to grommet table	⇨	Cart	2	0:16	1				
8	Delay	▽	Cart		2	1				
9	Attach grommet	◯	Grommet fastener		0.9	1				
10	Delay	▽	Cart		3	1				
11	Go to No. 1 inspection table	⇨	Cart	1	0.16	1				
12	No. 1 inspection	☐	Inspection table		5	2				
13	Delay	▽	Cart		2	1				
14	Go to finishing table	⇨	Cart	2	0.16	1				
15	Attach finish parts	◯	Cart		3	2				
16	Delay	▽	Cart		3	1				
17	Go to No. 2 inspection table	⇨	Cart	3	0.16	1				
18	No. 2 inspection	☐	Cart		5	2				
19	Delay	▽	Cart		60	1				
20	Transportation	⇨	Cart	5	—	1				
21	Storage	▽	Warehouse							
	Total	21 steps		19 m	135 min.	27 people	5 times (41.9 min.)	7 times (1.1 min.)	2 times (10 min.)	7 times (82 min.)

Figure 4-16. Product Process Chart (Before Improvement)

attachment do not take long and in fact are pretty well balanced in their processing times, we decided to remove the delay steps to improve the flow of operations. To do this, we combined processing tasks 5 through 8 into one transportation step and eliminated

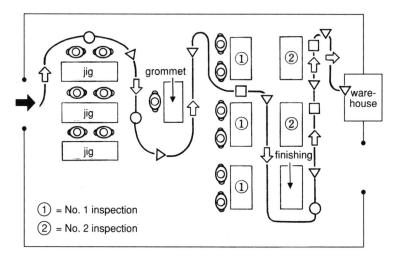

Figure 4-17. Flow Diagram (Before Improvement)

Table 4-8. Data Chart

	No. of Steps	Time (min.)	Distance (m)	People
Operation ○	5	41.9	—	9
Transportation ⇨	7	1.1	19	8
Inspection □	2	10	—	4
Delay ▽	7	82	—	6
Total	21	135	19	27

the delay steps listed as task numbers 10 and 16 in Figure 4-16.
2. We also decided to change the orientation of the table used for inspection No. 1 and move the finishing table to improve the flow.

The flow diagram for this improvement plan is shown in Figure 4-18 and the product process chart in Figure 4-19. Table 4-9 shows a comparison of measurements before the improvement and as specified in the improvement plan. If successful, the improvement plan promised to get rid of virtually all work-in-process delays and thereby achieve big reductions in labor-hours lost to retention and processing time. We recognized that the plan might also improve the flow of processes and shorten production lead time.

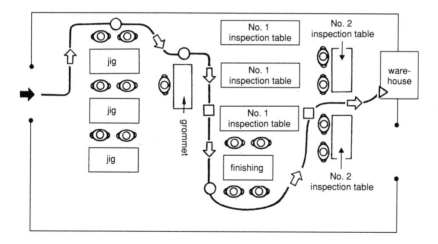

Figure 4-18. Flow Diagram (Improvement Plan)

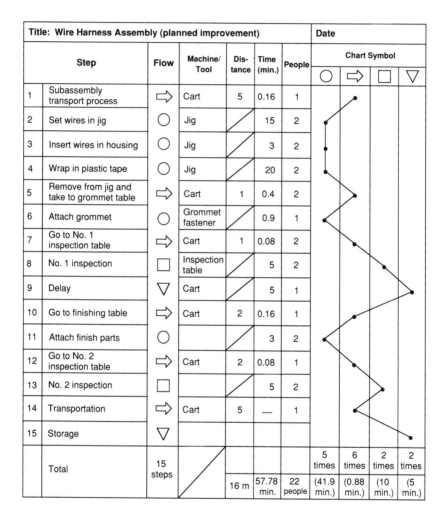

Title: Wire Harness Assembly (planned improvement)							Date			
Step		Flow	Machine/ Tool	Dis-tance	Time (min.)	People	Chart Symbol			
							○	⇨	☐	▽
1	Subassembly transport process	⇨	Cart	5	0.16	1				
2	Set wires in jig	○	Jig		15	2				
3	Insert wires in housing	○	Jig		3	2				
4	Wrap in plastic tape	○	Jig		20	2				
5	Remove from jig and take to grommet table	⇨	Cart	1	0.4	2				
6	Attach grommet	○	Grommet fastener		0.9	1				
7	Go to No. 1 inspection table	⇨	Cart	1	0.08	2				
8	No. 1 inspection	☐	Inspection table		5	2				
9	Delay	▽	Cart		5	1				
10	Go to finishing table	⇨	Cart	2	0.16	1				
11	Attach finish parts	○			3	2				
12	Go to No. 2 inspection table	⇨	Cart	2	0.08	1				
13	No. 2 inspection	☐			5	2				
14	Transportation	⇨	Cart	5	—	1				
15	Storage	▽								
	Total	15 steps		16 m	57.78 min.	22 people	5 times (41.9 min.)	6 times (0.88 min.)	2 times (10 min.)	2 times (5 min.)

Figure 4-19. Product Process Chart (Improvement Plan)

Step 6: Implement and evaluate the improvement plan

The effects of the improvement plan are illustrated in Figure 4-20.

Table 4-9. Comparison of Current Conditions with Planned Improvement

Step		Before Improvement	Improvement Plan	Net Reduction
Operation	No. of times	5	9	0
	Time (min.)	41.9	49.9	0
	Distance (m)	—	—	—
	People	9	9	0
Transpor-tation	No. of times	7	6	1
	Time (min.)	1.1	0.88	1.02
	Distance (m)	19	16	3
	People	8	8	0
Inspection	No. of times	2	2	0
	Time (min.)	10	10	0
	Distance (m)	—	—	—
	People	4	4	0
Retention	No. of times	7	2	5
	Time (min.)	82	5	77
	Distance (m)	—	—	—
	People	6	1	5
Total	No. of times	21	15	6
	Time (min.)	135	57.78	77.22
	Distance (m)	19	16	3
	People	27	22	5

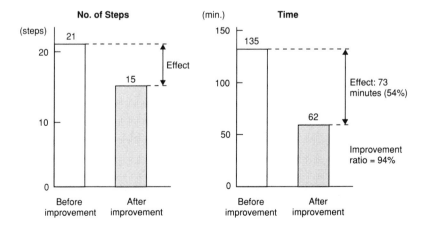

Figure 4-20. Effect of Improvement

Step 7: Standardize the improvement plan

The supervisors and shop-floor workers got together to carry out steps 6 and 7, which involved moving around some equipment. After implementing the improvement plan, we were fortunate in that everything went smoothly with no equipment breakdowns; the effects of the improvement were about as good as we had hoped. Our attainment rate for the overall production time goal came to 94 percent. The attainment rate is defined as the measured effect of the improvement (73 minutes) divided by the predicted effect of the improvement (77.2 minutes) multiplied by 100.

Problems on the Horizon

The improvement plan described above was an equipment layout improvement that did not require much time or money to implement. For the future, we would like to carry out more far-reaching improvements that include improved fabrication methods and greater mechanization and automation of the production processes.

CASE STUDY 3

Eliminating the Hole-punching Task in Coil Pressure Foot Fabrication
Report by: Shigeru Niikura, Meidensha KK, Production Headquarters

---

Reason for Making Improvement

After reading an article in our company's IE newsletter about improving the coil pressure foot process (see the case summary in Figure 4-21), I realized it might be possible to eliminate the entire hole-punching operation in our coil pressure foot fabrication process. I took up the matter with one of the factory supervisors and then decided to carry out a product process analysis.

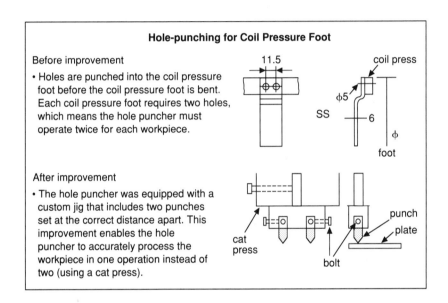

Hole-punching for Coil Pressure Foot

Before improvement

• Holes are punched into the coil pressure foot before the coil pressure foot is bent. Each coil pressure foot requires two holes, which means the hole puncher must operate twice for each workpiece.

After improvement

• The hole puncher was equipped with a custom jig that includes two punches set at the correct distance apart. This improvement enables the hole puncher to accurately process the workpiece in one operation instead of two (using a cat press).

Figure 4-21. Case Summary from IE Newsletter Article

Outline of Processes

Our company turns out about 50 units per month of the product using the coil pressure feet that are the focus of this improvement; each unit uses 12 coil pressure feet. Figure 4-22 shows the material used for this part and the part's final shape. Figure 4-23 shows a flow diagram of the processes at our plant where these parts are manufactured.

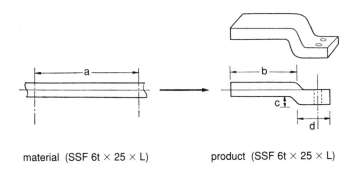

material (SSF 6t × 25 × L)   product (SSF 6t × 25 × L)

Figure 4-22. Material and Shape of Part

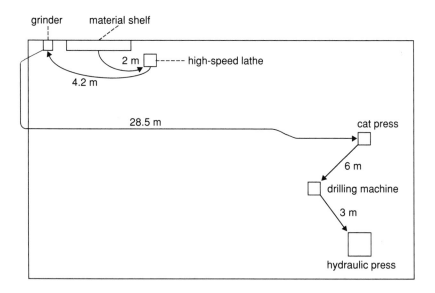

Figure 4-23. Flow Diagram

Product Process Analysis

Step 1: Conduct a preliminary study

As the process outline shows, our preliminary study clarified the production yield, material and product shapes, and process flow, and revealed that there are 14 steps between delivery of the workpiece materials and retention of the finished products ready to be shipped.

Step 2: Draw up a process flow chart

Figure 4-24 shows our product process chart, including a process flow chart.

Step 3: Gather necessary data for the analysis

See the measurement in Figure 4-24.

Step 4: Organize the analysis results

Table 4-10 shows the table in which we organized our results.

Step 5: Draft an improvement plan

Our analysis revealed that processing accounted for almost all (96.9 percent) of the production time, while transportation came to only 1 percent and inspection totaled a mere 2.1 percent. We wondered if it might be possible to combine three particular operations: marking, punching, and drilling. We considered using a push plate to do this.

Assuming that our plan to combine these three processes was feasible, we drew up another product process chart based on such a plan. This chart is shown in Figure 4-25.

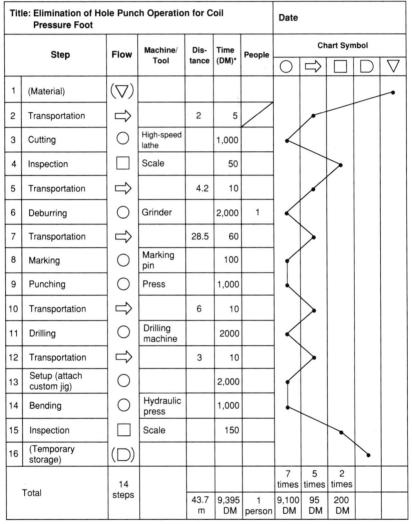

	Title: Elimination of Hole Punch Operation for Coil Pressure Foot					Date					
	Step	Flow	Machine/ Tool	Dis- tance	Time (DM)*	People	Chart Symbol				
							◯	⇨	☐	𝔻	▽
1	(Material)	(▽)									•
2	Transportation	⇨		2	5						
3	Cutting	◯	High-speed lathe		1,000		•				
4	Inspection	☐	Scale		50				•		
5	Transportation	⇨		4.2	10			•			
6	Deburring	◯	Grinder		2,000	1	•				
7	Transportation	⇨		28.5	60			•			
8	Marking	◯	Marking pin		100		•				
9	Punching	◯	Press		1,000		•				
10	Transportation	⇨		6	10			•			
11	Drilling	◯	Drilling machine		2000		•				
12	Transportation	⇨		3	10			•			
13	Setup (attach custom jig)	◯			2,000		•				
14	Bending	◯	Hydraulic press		1,000		•				
15	Inspection	☐	Scale		150				•		
16	(Temporary storage)	(𝔻)								•	
	Total	14 steps					7 times	5 times	2 times		
				43.7 m	9,395 DM	1 person	9,100 DM	95 DM	200 DM		

* Decimal minutes

Figure 4-24. Product Process Chart (Before Improvement)

Table 4-10. Data Chart

		No. of Steps	Time (DM)*	Distance (m)	People
Operation	○	7	9,100	——	1
Transportation	⇨	5	95	43.7	(1)
Inspection	▢	2	200	——	(1)
Retention	▽	——	——	——	——
Total		14	9,395	43.7	1

*Decimal minutes

Step 6: Evaluate the improvement plan

Table 4-11 shows a comparison of measurements made before the improvement and predicted effects of the improvement plan. As the table indicates, the plan was expected to achieve a 12.1 percent reduction in processing time and a 10.5 percent cut in transportation time.

Suggestions for the Future

1. *Processing:* We proposed the adoption of a push plate to combine processes (and thereby achieve a 12.1 percent cut in processing time).
2. *Inspection:* The inspection measurements at points *a* and *b* (shown in Figure 4-22) can be made with a scale, but we suggested that the inspectors switch to another measurement tool that would probably save time.
3. *Standardization:* The coil pressure feet are made in various dimensions to match different types of equipment. If it is possible to make the hole sizes and positions the same for all types, we could use the same push plate for all the coil pressure feet. We asked the design department to look into it.

	Step	Flow	Machine/Tool	Dis-tance	Time (DM)*	People	Chart Symbol
Title: Elimination of Hole Punch Operation for Coil Pressure Foot							Date
1	(Material)	(▽)					
2	Transportation	⇨		2	5		
3	Cutting	○	High-speed lathe		1,000		
4	Inspection	□	Scale		50		
5	Transportation	⇨		4.2	10		
6	Deburring	○	Grinder		2,000	1	
7	Transportation	⇨		28.5	60		
8	Drilling	○	Marking pin		2,000		
9	Transportation	⇨	Press	3	10		
10	Setup	○			2,000		
11	Bending	○	Drilling machine		1,000		
12	Inspection	□			150		
13	(Temporary storage)	(D)					
Total		11 steps		37.7 m	8,285 DM	1 person	5 times / 8,000 DM	4 times / 85 DM	2 times / 200 DM

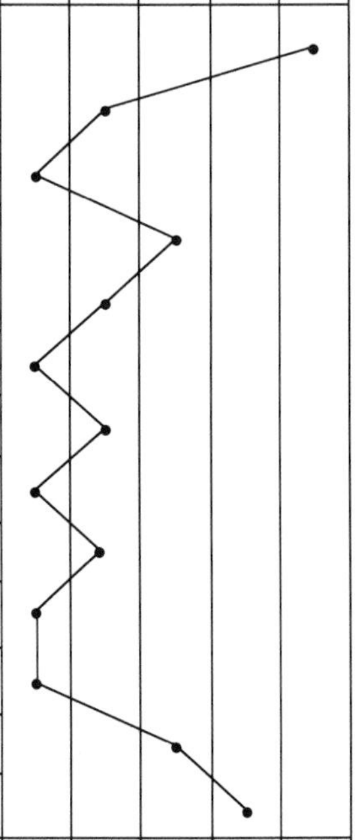

* Decimal minutes

Figure 4-25. Product Process Chart (Improvement Plan)

4. *Transportation routes:* The transportation distance is particularly long between the grinder and the cat press. We asked the factory supervisors to consider changing the layout to shorten this transportation distance as long as it does not cause problems for other products.

Table 4-11. Comparison of Current Conditions with Planned Improvement

	Operation			Transportation			Inspection			Total		
	Before Improvement	Improvement Plan	Net Reduction (%)	Before Improvement	Improvement Plan	Net Reduction (%)	Before Improvement	Improvement Plan	Net Reduction (%)	Before Improvement	Improvement Plan	Net Reduction (%)
No. of Steps	7	5	28.6	5	4	20	2	2	0	14	11	21.4
Time (DM)	9,100	8,000	12.1	95	85	10.5	200	200	0	9,395	8,285	11.8
Distance (m)	—	—	—	43.7	37.7	13.7	—	—	—	43.7	37.7	13.7

Conclusion

The factory supervisors adopted suggestions 1 and 2. In fact, they found that using the push plates and the inspection measurement tool brought about major savings in labor-hours, and the production engineers decided to promote the use of these new jigs and tools in other lines at the factory.

The design department adopted suggestion 3. They were already busy carrying out a group technology analysis for all the machine types, and when they considered unifying the size and position of the holes in the coil pressure feet, they found it could be done and standardized the new design.

The factory managers responded to suggestion 4 by moving the long transportation route to another location so it could be shortened. This change was probably the result of a "path analysis" of the transportation system at the factory.

As described above, our product process analysis led to an improvement plan that brought substantial improvements in various areas and, in particular, better operations in the targeted production line.

5

Operator Process Analysis

WHAT IS OPERATOR PROCESS ANALYSIS?

Operator process analysis is an analytical method by which you study a sequence of operation-related tasks performed by the operator, plot them on a process analysis chart, find where problems exist within those tasks, and make the needed improvements.

These analytical methods are almost identical to the ones described in the Chapter 4 discussion of product process analysis. Only the object of study — operators rather than products — is different. This focus on the operator means that the process analysis will have a narrower and more detailed focus.

The symbols used for operator process analysis are shown in Table 5-1. The supplementary symbols and symbol combinations are similar to those used in product process analysis.

THE PURPOSE OF OPERATOR PROCESS ANALYSIS

Although product process analysis follows the flow of goods through processes and operator process analysis follows

Table 5-1. Operator Process Chart Symbols

Step	Symbol	Meaning	Comments
Operation	◯	Any action that alters the shape or other characteristic of a material, part, or product. This includes setup operations for processing and inspection.	
Inspection	☐ ◇	Indicates either volume inspection or quality inspection	
Transpor-tation	⇨	Indicates any action that moves objects (including one's own body) from one place to another	Some chartmakers use the arrow exclusively for moving without carrying a load (conveyance), and note carrying a load (transport) with a small circle.
Delay	▽	Indicates delays while waiting for materials or for the comple-tion of conveyance trips and/or automatic processing	

the flow of the operator's work in processes, the analytical approach taken in each case is almost the same.

Operator process analysis is a useful method for studying the work done by operators who move from place to place as they work and for finding and eliminating the Big 3 problems as they exist in such work. As in product process analysis, it is important to follow the four basic principles of improvement (see Table 2-3) as you look for

- unnecessary delay points along the line,
- unnecessary transportation trips,
- unnecessarily long transportation distances,
- problems posed by the choice of transportation method, and
- opportunities to combine operations and inspection,

while studying ways to improve

- the equipment layout,
- the sequence of work, and
- the distribution of workloads

to determine whether there is a better way of doing things.

STEPS IN OPERATOR PROCESS ANALYSIS

Operator process analysis uses the same steps as in product process analysis. As a simple example, take a look at the steps for analyzing the setup operations for the morning commute to work — the sequence that begins with waking up and ends with leaving the house.

Step 1: Conduct a Preliminary Study

As in product process analysis, start by asking around and reading up on the facts concerning the current production conditions, such as the state of the equipment, the layout, process flow, raw materials, and products. In operator process analysis, it is especially important to find out how proficient the operators are at their work and to use someone of average proficiency as the object of analysis.

Step 2: Draw Up a Process Flow Chart

Create a flow chart using the process chart symbols shown in Table 5-1, following the flow of the activities. When doing this, carefully consider the purpose of each step within the various categories of operations, transportation, inspection, and delays.

Within the actual flow of activities, there may be places where it is difficult to clearly define where operations stop and transportation begins. It is important not to be vague in this area, however, since failures in clearly defining start and end points can develop into obstructions later in the analysis. Therefore, be very careful and accurate when drawing the line between one step and the next.

Figure 5-1 shows an operator process chart as it might be drawn to describe the flow of operations involved in preparing to go to work in the morning.

Step 3: Record Measurements for All Required Items in Each Process

Once you have drawn a flow chart, you need to measure various items in each process and record the measurements on a table. Make measurements while observing the operator as he or she is doing the work.

1. You may want to use a preprinted worksheet such as the operator process chart shown in Figure 5-1.
2. As with the product process chart (see Table 4-1), list each of the measurement items in a grid. Be sure to enter the required time and the transportation distance. Use the appropriate space to record the names of various machines, equipment jigs, sites, and other such items included in the analysis.
3. Generally, the unit of analysis is the lot size defined by the number of products made by the operator in one cycle of operations. Unless you establish such a unit of analysis, you will not be able to obtain a required time measurement for each unit, which will make it impossible to compare the required times of various processes.
4. Figure 5-2 shows a flow diagram of the steps performed by the person in this case.

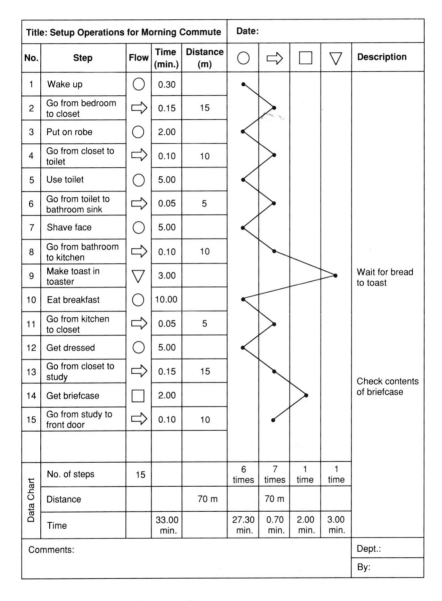

Title: Setup Operations for Morning Commute					Date:					
No.	Step	Flow	Time (min.)	Distance (m)	○	⇨	□	▽	Description
1	Wake up	○	0.30						
2	Go from bedroom to closet	⇨	0.15	15					
3	Put on robe	○	2.00						
4	Go from closet to toilet	⇨	0.10	10					
5	Use toilet	○	5.00						
6	Go from toilet to bathroom sink	⇨	0.05	5					
7	Shave face	○	5.00						
8	Go from bathroom to kitchen	⇨	0.10	10					
9	Make toast in toaster	▽	3.00						Wait for bread to toast
10	Eat breakfast	○	10.00						
11	Go from kitchen to closet	⇨	0.05	5					
12	Get dressed	○	5.00						
13	Go from closet to study	⇨	0.15	15					
14	Get briefcase	□	2.00						Check contents of briefcase
15	Go from study to front door	⇨	0.10	10					
Data Chart	No. of steps	15			6 times	7 times	1 time	1 time	
	Distance			70 m		70 m			
	Time		33.00 min.		27.30 min.	0.70 min.	2.00 min.	3.00 min.	
Comments:									Dept.:
									By:

Figure 5-1. Operator Process Chart

(a) Flow Diagram (Before Improvement)

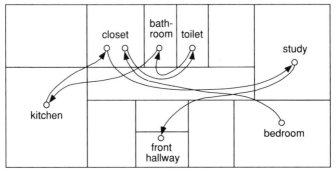

(b) Flow Diagram (Improvement Plan)

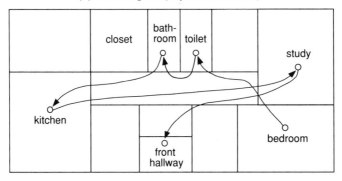

Figure 5-2. Before and After Flow Diagrams

Step 4: Organize the Analysis Results

After recording your measurements in the product process chart shown in Figure 5-1, add up the column data on the bottom part of the chart. In this case, there are a total of 15 steps (6 operations, 7 transportation trips, 1 inspection, and 1 delay), a total time of 33 minutes (27.3 minutes for operations, 0.7 for transportation, 2.0 for inspection, and 3.0 for delays), and a total transportation distance of 70 meters.

Your objectives now are to find ways to minimize all transportation, inspection, and delays that are not absolutely required for the operations, and then to make the operations themselves easier and faster.

Step 5: Draft an Improvement Plan

Using your product process chart with the data chart at the bottom (Figure 5-1) and the flow diagram (Figure 5-2), you are now ready to pick out the problem points and start devising improvements to solve the problems. At this point, it is very important to solicit input from as many people as possible. You may want to refer back to Table 4-3, which lists the various improvement ideas generated for the product process analysis example discussed there.

In this example, the brainstorming session produced the following problem points:

1. There are too many transportation trips. (Since they are in a small house, these extra trips do not add much time to the total, but in a factory they would add much more.)
2. Look for a way to eliminate the inspection process (checking the contents of the briefcase).
3. Look for a way to eliminate the delay (waiting for the toaster to toast the bread).
4. You might also ask whether it is really necessary for the person to go to another room to get a robe and then change into work clothes, all within a short time frame.
5. Look for ways to reduce the time required for using the toilet, shaving, eating, and dressing.

After considering these points, you might come up with the following improvement proposals:

a. Instead of going to the closet to get a robe, the person should keep it by the bed and just slip it on after he or she gets out of bed.
b. If the chest of drawers is placed in the study, the person will not have to use the closet at all in the morning.

    c. If the person checks the contents of his or her briefcase the night before, he or she can avoid that inspection process in the morning.

    d. If the person's spouse can make the toast, he or she can eliminate the waiting time.

    e. The above improvements would reduce the number of transportation trips.

    f. A motion study might uncover ways to shorten the time required for using the toilet, shaving, eating, and dressing, but we have decided against doing such a study in this case.

Figure 5-3 and part (b) of the flow diagram shown in Figure 5-2 describe the improvement plan based on the above proposals. As you can see, the plan reduces the number of processes and streamlines the process flow.

Next, compare the current conditions with the expected results of the improvement plan, using a comparison table such as that shown in Table 5-2. In this case, the improvement plan eliminates 5 steps (including the one inspection and one delay), 7.15 minutes, and 2 transportation trips. In terms of total time, the effect of the improvement is to save the person 7 minutes each morning as he or she gets ready to go to work.

Step 6: Implement and Evaluate the Improvement Plan

Once your improvement plan has been approved, you can implement it. If you are using any new work methods, be sure to provide for adequate training to make up for inexperience. Measure and evaluate the improvement's results only after the workers have become proficient in the new methods. Promptly and affirmatively address any abnormalities that appear during implementation.

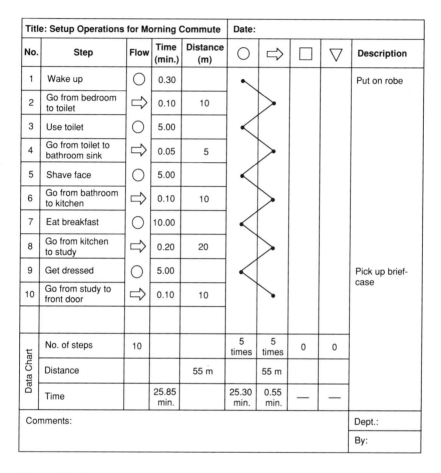

Figure 5-3. Operator Process Chart (Improvement Plan)

Step 7: Standardize the Improvement Plan

If the evaluation shows that the improvement plan has produced the predicted results, do not hesitate to standardize the improvement to prevent backsliding. Remember, no improvement plan is perfect, and there is always room for further improvement via follow-up measures.

Table 5-2. Comparison of Current Conditions with Planned Improvement

Step	No. of Steps			Time (min.)			Distance (m)		
	Before Improvement	Improvement Plan	Effect	Before Improvement	Improvement Plan	Effect	Before Improvement	Improvement Plan	Effect
Operation	6	5	1	27.30	25.30	2.00	—	—	—
Transportation	7	5	2	0.70	0.55	0.15	70	55	15
Inspection	1	0	1	2.00	0	2.00	—	—	—
Delay	1	0	1	3.00	0	3.00	—	—	—
Total	15	10	5	33.00	25.85	7.15	70	55	15

EXAMPLES OF OPERATOR PROCESS ANALYSIS

The following case studies of operator process analysis were selected from fieldwork reports submitted by students in JUSE's FIE seminar.

The first case study concerns layout and equipment improvements that resulted in simpler operations and a more efficient flow of work. The second case study concerns a work changeover improvement that was very effective in reducing transportation trips, shortening the transportation distance, and saving overall time. The new work procedures were standardized to prevent mistakes and this resulted in much higher operational reliability.

Keep these case studies in mind as you reappraise the conditions at your workplace. If each person becomes more problem-conscious and takes a closer look at the workplace, everyone will be sure to find similar needs for improvement.

CASE STUDY 1

**Improving Setup through Operator Process Analysis
Report by: Hiroshi Ito, Takeda Pharmaceuticals Co.,
    Konan Plant**

Overview

At our factory, we have a filtering process for removing foreign particles and other impurities from water. There are various kinds of setup operations for this process, each involving different tools and pipes that must be assembled in rather complicated ways. Any delay in completing these setup procedures has a big impact on the changeover operations for the next process. Therefore, we need to find a way to make these first setup operations go more smoothly and reliably.

We began our improvement effort by performing an operator process analysis of the current conditions. Specifically, we studied the following improvement needs:

1. Minimizing operation motion and raising efficiency
2. Improving equipment layout and making work easier
3. Standardizing the flow of work

In view of these needs, we came up with the following improvement proposals:

a. Change the shape of the devices.
b. Consolidate the workshop.
c. Minimize device assembly to make work easier.

We estimated that these improvements would shorten the overall operation time from the current 17 minutes and 30 seconds to just 7 minutes and 17 seconds, and that it would make the work involved in getting production started both easier and smoother.

Description of Filter Setup Operation

Figure 5-4 illustrates the processes involved in the filter setup operation.

Analysis of Current Conditions

We carried out an operator process analysis of the setup operations for the filtering process, following the prescribed steps. Specifically, we did the following:

1. Made a preliminary study
2. Drew up a process flow chart
3. Recorded measurements for all required items in each process
4. Organized the analysis results

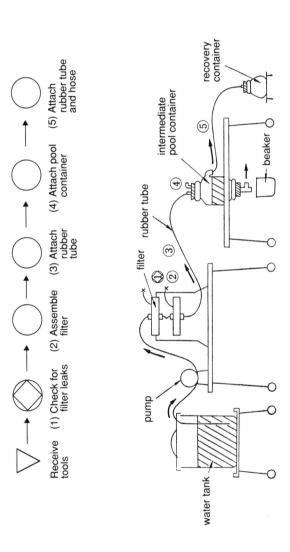

Figure 5-4. Setup Operations for Filtering Process

Our flow diagram is shown in Figure 5-5, and our operator process chart is shown in Figure 5-6. After studying these, we came up with the following improvement points:

1. There are ten transportation trips within just one setup operation (this accounts for 43.5 percent of total operation time). This is clearly too much transportation.
2. There is too much moving around between the two rooms.
3. The flow of operations is not smooth. Layout changes are needed to address these first three improvement points.
4. There is too much to do within the given total operation time.
5. The work methods differ from one worker to the next.

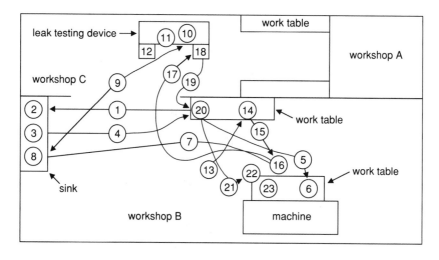

Figure 5-5. Flow Diagram (Current Conditions)

Improvement Plan Based on the Preliminary Study

Our improvement plan based on the preliminary study called for three improvement actions.

Object of Analysis: Setup Operations						Dept. A		Team A
No.	Description	Opera-tion	Transpor-tation	Inspec-tion	Delay	Dis-tance	Time (sec.)	Improvement Ideas
1	Carry filter from work table to sink					4	3	
2	Set up containers						3	
3	Wash out containers						60	Can this be done during free time beforehand?
4	Get work table and recovery container					6	5	
5	Carry recovery container to work table next to machine					1	1	
6	Set up recovery container and connect tube						120	
7	Get filter from sink					5	4	
8	Drain sink						30	
9	Carry filter to leak test table					10	8	Leak test device needs to be installed next to machine.
10	Start air flow						3	
11	Test for leaks						60	
12	Check air pressure						6	
13	Get intermediate container from work table					5	4	What if a pre-assembly intermediate container were used instead of the pool-type one currently being used?
14	Assemble intermediate container						20	
15	Move intermediate container to other work table					1	1	
16	Set up intermediate container						40	
17	Get filter					10	10	Same as steps 9 through 11
18	Check air pressure						6	
19	Carry filter to work table					10	10	
20	Drain water from filter						180	
21	Carry filter to work table next to machine					1	1	
22	Assemble filter						120	Leave it assembled
23	Connect filter tubes						360	
Data Chart	No. of Steps	11	10	2	0	Total		
	Time	996	47	12	0	Time	Distance	People
	People					1055	53	

Figure 5-6. Operator Process Chart (Current Conditions)

1. Improve the layout
2. Improve the tools
3. Improve the work methods

Table 5-3 lists the contents of the improvement plan. Figure 5-7 illustrates an example of the tool improvements that we made. Figure 5-8 shows the operator process chart of our improvement, and Figure 5-9 shows the corresponding flow diagram.

Table 5-3. Improvement Plan

Major Improvement Actions	Estimated Effect on Operations
1. Move all of the work in workshop C to workshop B to shorten the conveyance distance (see the flow diagram in Figure 5-6).	
• Move the leak testing device to the work table in workshop B (where the roller pump and filter are).	• Reduce transportation from steps ⑩,⑪, and [12] in flow diagram.
• Reduce the number of trips to the sink.	• Reduce transportation from steps ②,③, and ⑧ in flow diagram.
• Move the air pressure gauge from workshop C to the side of the machine in workshop B.	• Facilitate operation at step [12] in flow diagram.
2. Rinse out the filter only once.	• Reduce operation time at step ③ in flow diagram.
3. Leave the tools assembled.	• Reduce operation time at step ⑭ in flow diagram.
4. Change the shape of the intermediate container.	• Simplify operation at step ⑯ in flow diagram.
5. Change the filtering method.	• Reduce the number of operations at steps ⑭, ⑮, and ⑯ in flow diagram.
6. Unify the sequence of operation methods and reduce the amount of work.	• Reduce total number of steps to 9 (keep a standard sequence of operations that cannot be changed while in progress).

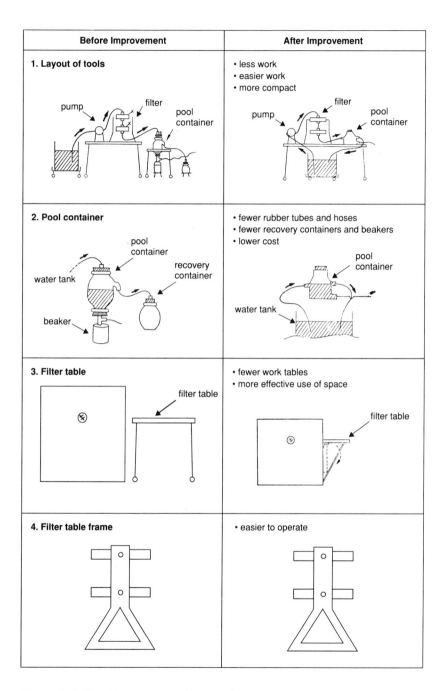

Before Improvement	After Improvement
1. Layout of tools	• less work • easier work • more compact
2. Pool container	• fewer rubber tubes and hoses • fewer recovery containers and beakers • lower cost
3. Filter table	• fewer work tables • more effective use of space
4. Filter table frame	• easier to operate

Figure 5-7. Tool Improvement Example

Object of Analysis: Setup Operations						Dept. A		Team A
No.	Description	Opera-tion	Trans-portation	Inspec-tion	Delay	Distance (m)	Time	Improvement Ideas
1	Start air flow	○	○	□	▽		3	
2	Test for leaks	○	○	□	▽		60	• Reduced transporta-tion distance
3	Check air pressure gauge	○	○	□	▽		6	• Two filters can be handled in one place.
4	Go get filter set	○	○	□	▽	1	1	
5	Carry filter set to work table	○	○	□	▽	1	1	• All operations are done in one workshop.
6	Set up filter set	○	○	□	▽		60	
7	Check air pressure gauge	○	○	□	▽		6	
8	Drain water from filter	○	○	□	▽		180	
9	Connect tubes	○	○	□	▽		120	
Data Chart		No. of Steps	5	2	2	0	Total	
		Time	423	2	12	0	Time (s)	Distance (m)	People
		People					437	2	

Figure 5-8. Operator Process Chart (After Improvement)

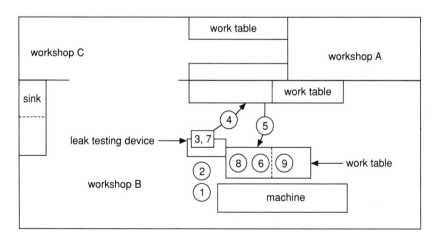

Figure 5-9. Flow Diagram (After Improvement)

Evaluation

1. The improvement reduced the amount of work while raising production capacity. As Table 5-4 shows, a 618-second reduction in total operation time enabled us to raise the equipment utilization rate, which in turn is expected to make possible a higher production capacity.

Table 5-4. Results of Improvement

	Before improvement	After improvement	Effect
Operation time	1,055 seconds	437 seconds	618 seconds less
Steps	23	9	14 fewer steps

2. Improving the filtering method enabled us to reduce the variety of tools needed, which is expected to lower costs.
3. If we can redistribute the work to allow for prior assembly of the tools, we can reduce time spent on assembly and alleviate some of the fatigue caused by the heavy work load in these setup operations.
4. We reduced the number of transportation trips and improved the layout.
5. We changed the work methods to make them simpler, safer, and more error-proof.

Required Equipment

Table 5-5 lists the equipment required for this improvement and various cost estimates.

Conclusion and Future Plans

As a result of the improvement we made using the IE methods we learned in this seminar, we were able to do even

Table 5-5. Required Equipment and Related Costs (Estimated)

	Specification	No. required	Cost (estimated)	
			Unit cost	Total
Fabrication of filter table	Fold-out table alongside machine	1	$630	$630
Frame for filter	One frame re-modeled for easier use	2	48	96
Transfer of leak test table	Moved from work-shop C to work-shop B	1 (done by improvement team, using pipe parts)	5.50	5.50
Improvement of filter	Bolts attached to side of filter	2 (done by improvement team)	5.50	11.00
(conversion rate: ¥135/$1.00)		Total	Approx. $742.00	

better than we had expected in removing the Big 3 problems from our filter setup operations. Previously, we had been at a total loss when searching for the cause of our productivity problems; now we have a rational and easy method for pinpointing problems in the workshop. We are happy to know that any improvement plan that uses the operator process analysis method can be expected to bring benefits such as higher capacity, greater stability, standardization, and simplification to the factory.

For the future, we plan to consider the following remaining issues:

1. We want to look into ways of gaining fuller understanding from all operators about the implementation of improvements.
2. We want to work out a more efficient distribution of work with other processes to improve the work balance and the overall process flow.
3. We want to follow up on these improvements with quality and improvements.

CASE STUDY 2

Operator Process Analysis for Layering Work
Report by: Kenji Toiyama, Asahi Glass Co., Keihin Plant

Overview

In our workshop, work is centered on glass-layering processes, which required a lot of labor-hours and had high costs. We decided to carry out an operator process analysis of this layering work (using heat lights and wire full decker switches) and then came up with a cost-saving improvement plan. Our improvement resulted in elimination of 11 steps, 40 meters of transportation, and 1 minute and 20 seconds of operation cycle time.

Outline of Operation Processes

The work process that we targeted for improvement was an intermediate process for making antifog glass. In this process, we stretch heating-wire coils across a middle sheet, then attach electrodes and terminals to the wires and heat-press the wires and middle sheet between two plates of glass. Figure 5-10 illustrates this process.

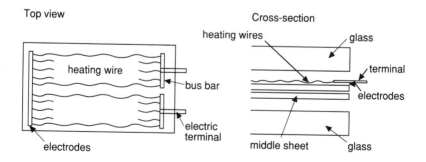

Figure 5-10. Lamination Process Operations

Operator Process Analysis

Analysis of current conditions

Following the specified operator process analysis steps, we made a preliminary study of current conditions. Our findings are shown in the flow diagram in Figure 5-11 and the operator process chart in Figure 5-12.

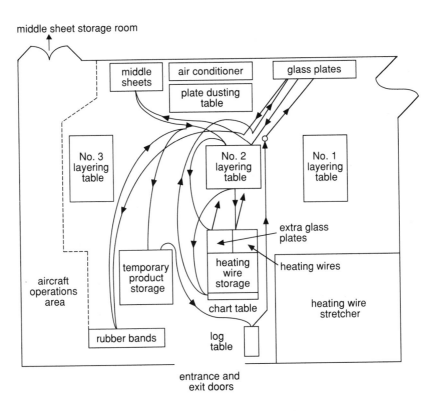

Figure 5-11. Flow Diagram (Before Improvement)

As the operator process chart shows, this process included 19 operations, 18 transportation trips, and 1 inspection. We were particularly impressed with how many transportation trips the

Title: Layering Operation (Heating Wires)   Date:

No.	Step	Flow	Time (sec.)	Dis-tance	◯	o	□	▽	Description
1	Layering table	◯							• Set up for layering
2		o	7	3.8					
3	Glass plate pile	◯							• Bring glass plate
4		o	7	3.8					
5	Layering table	◯							• Put down glass plate and dust it off
6		o	9	4.6					
7	Middle sheet roller	◯							• Measure and cut middle sheet
8		o	9	4.6					
9	Layering table	◯							• Set middle sheet on top of glass plate
10		o							
11	Cut middle sheet	◯							• Trim middle sheet to match glass plate's dimensions
12		o	7	3.1					
13	Middle sheet remnant pile	◯							• Put down middle sheet
14		o	7	3.1					
15	Layering table	◯							• Dust off middle sheet
16		o	7	3.1					
17	Heating wire storage	◯							• Stretch heating wires across middle sheet
18		o	7	3.1					
19	Layering table	◯							• Set middle sheet back on top of glass plate
20		o	12	5.2					
21	Chart table	□							• Check chart
22		o	12	5.2					
23	Process heating wires	◯							• Attach bus bar terminals and attach to wires
24		o	7	3.8					
25	Glass plate pile	◯							• Dust off another glass plate and bring it to layering table
26		o	7	3.8					
27	Layering table	◯							• Align two glass plates and trim off any protruding middle sheet
28		◯							
29		o	17	9.5					
30	Rubber band pile	◯							• Pick up a rubber band
31		o	17	9.5					
32	Layering table	◯							• Cut tape and put a rubber band around the glass plates
33		o	10	5.0					
34	Temporary product storage	◯							• Set glass plates on a cart
35		o	8	3.6					
36	Log table	◯							• Record operation time, middle sheet dimensions
37		o	15	6.3					
38	Layering table	◯							• Set up for next process
Summary	Steps	38			19	18	1	0	
	Distance (m)			81.1					
	Time (sec.)		165						

Figure 5-12. Operator Process Chart (Before Improvement)

process had. Even though these trips were mainly just to pick up glass plates and a rubber band, they ate up most of the operation cycle time; the operations and inspection consumed relatively little time.

The flow diagram shows that the operator has to walk a very complicated course that totals 81 meters of transportation distance. Clearly, there was a need to reduce the number of trips and shorten the transportation distance.

Drafting of improvement plan

In response to the excessive transportation trips exposed by the operator process analysis, we sought ways to reduce the number of operations, the number of transportation trips, and the transportation distance, thereby shortening the operation cycle time and raising productivity. We came up with the following improvement ideas, and made the improvements:

1. We remodeled the rubber band carts so that the rubber bands could be kept close at hand, thereby reducing the transportation distance (see Figure 5-13).
2. We set up a new storage area for the middle sheets and had the middle sheets precut for use in this process (see Figure 5-14).

The operator process chart and flow diagram describing the process according to the improvement plan are shown in Figures 5-15 and 5-16.

Evaluation of improvement plan

Table 5-6 shows a comparison of this process before and after improvement. As shown in the table, the improvement eliminated 40 meters from the total transportation distance and 1 minute and 20 seconds from the operation cycle time.

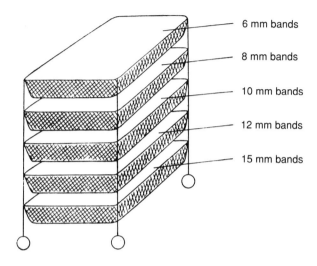

Figure 5-13. Remodeled Rubber Band Cart

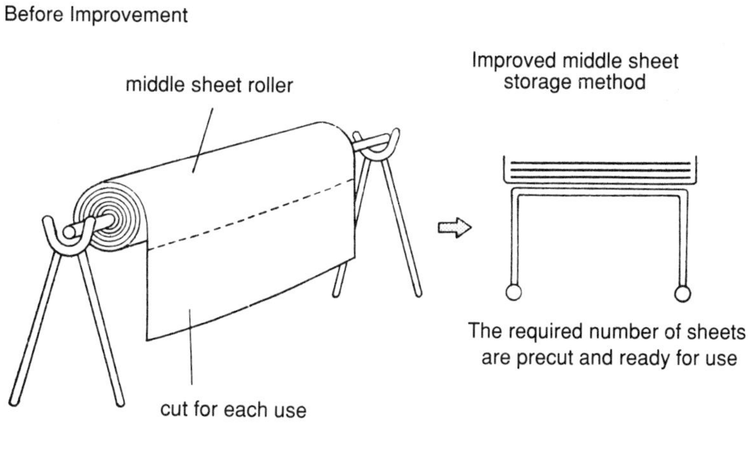

Before Improvement

middle sheet roller

Improved middle sheet
storage method

⇨

cut for each use

The required number of sheets
are precut and ready for use

**Figure 5-14. New Storage Site for Middle Sheets and Change to
Precut Sheets (After Improvement)**

No.	Step	Flow	Time (sec.)	Dis-tance	○	○	□	▽	Description
	Title: Layering Operation (Heating Wires)								Date:
1	Layering table	○							• Set up for layering
2		○	7	3.8					
3	Glass plate pile	○							• Get glass plate
4		○	7	3.8					
5	Layering table	○							• Dust off glass plate
6		○	9	4.6					
7	Middle sheet cart	○							• Bring middle sheet
8		○	9	4.6					
9	Layering table	○							• Set middle sheet on plate
10		○							
11	Heating wire storage	○							
12		○	7	3.1					
13	Layering table	○							
14	Check charts	□	7	3.1					• Check position and quantity of wires, etc.
15	Process heating wires	○							• Attach bus bar terminals and attach to wires
16		○	7	3.1					
17	Glass plate pile	○							• Dust off another glass plate and bring it to layering table
18		○	7	3.1					
19	Layering table	○							• Align two glass plates and trim off any protruding middle sheet
20		○	12	5.2					• Trim off any protruding middle sheet
21		○							
22		○	12	5.2					• Pick up a rubber band
23	Temporary product storage	○							• Set the glass plates on a cart
24		○	7	3.8					
25	Log book table	○							• Record operation time, middle sheet dimensions
26		○	7	3.8					
27	Layering table	○							• Set up for the next process
Summary	Steps	27			15	11	1		
	Distance (m)			41.1					
	Time (sec.)		85						

Figure 5-15. Operator Process Chart (Improvement Plan)

Layout Improvement

After studying the results of the above improvement, we also improved the workshop layout, as shown in Figure 5-17. The new layout removed wasteful motion and made the flow of operations smoother.

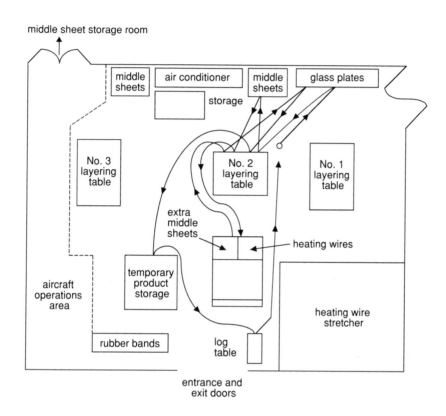

Figure 5-16. Flow Diagram (Improvement Plan)

Table 5-6. Comparison Table

	Before Improvement	After Improvement	Effect
No. of steps	38	27	11
Time (sec.)	165	85	80
Distance (m)	81.1	41.1	40.0

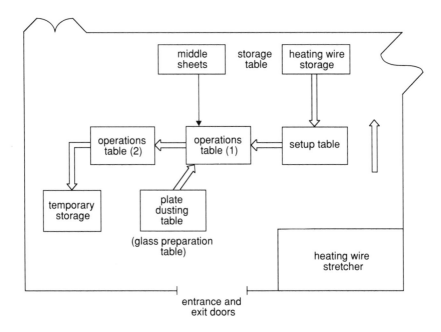

Figure 5-17. Improved Workshop Layout

Problems for the Future

In the future, we intend to carry out more operator process analyses to shorten our operation cycle times for various processes.

6

Joint Process Analysis

WHAT IS JOINT PROCESS ANALYSIS?

Factory processes are seldom simple enough to consist of a single operation done by a single operator. Most consist of various combinations of people and machines. The following combinations are often found in factories:

- One operator working with one machine
- One operator working with several machines
- Several people working together
- Several people working with one machine
- Several people working with several machines

Joint process analysis is an IE technique you can use to increase the efficiency of such operations, which usually contain a greater share of delays and obstacles than the simpler types of operations described so far. This type of analysis is sometimes referred to as *combined operation analysis*. It can be broken down further into *operator-machine analysis*, for studying operations involving at least one person and one machine, and *joint operation analysis,* for studying operations involving several people who work together.

Through time studies and diagrams of operational combinations of people or people and machines, joint process analysis reveals exactly where the idle time exists within such operations and facilitates improvements in work organization to eliminate waste.

The analytical methods used in joint process analysis differ somewhat from those employed in product and operator process analysis. For instance, joint process analysis uses some different process chart symbols, as shown in Table 6-1.

Table 6-1. Joint Process Chart Symbols

Operator Symbols		Machine Symbols	
Solitary	The operator's work has no temporal relation to any other operator's or machine's work.	Auto-matic	The machine operates automatically without any relation to operators.
Joint or assisted	The operator works with one or more other operators (joint operations) or one or more machines (assisted operations).	Assisted	The timing of the machine's operation is restricted by the timing of operator assistance, such as in changeover, or attaching or removing parts.
Delay (standby time)	The operator must wait until at least one machine or other operator is ready before continuing his or her work.	Idle time	The machine must wait until the operator is ready to assist it before it can continue its work.

Because joint process analysis includes elements of operator-machine analysis and joint operation analysis, it can be used with product process analysis and/or operator process analysis to obtain optimal results. After referring to Figure 3-1 for a general breakdown of process analysis into more specific types of analysis, select the most appropriate type of analysis for the type of process you are analyzing.

THE PURPOSE OF JOINT PROCESS ANALYSIS

The purpose of joint process analysis is to clarify the interrelationships between operators and machines or among several operators, to find where time may be wasted (as operator standby time or machine idle time) and to make corrective improvements. The goals of joint process analysis include

1. Eliminating machine idle time, thereby raising the capacity utilization rate
2. Eliminating operator standby time, thereby raising work efficiency (such as reducing labor requirements and/or raising worker productivity)
3. Equalizing the distribution of work among operators and machines
4. Assigning the optimal number of machines per operator
5. Assigning the optimal number of operators to joint operations

The overall goal is to get the work done using fewer operators and within a shorter time period while maintaining an even distribution of work. This combination of factors helps promote both productivity and an easier flow of operations.

OPERATOR-MACHINE ANALYSIS

What Is Operator-machine Analysis?

Operator-machine analysis is a way of studying the relation between the respective operating times of human operators and machines. When one person operates several machines, as for instance in machining lines, machines go idle when the operator is busy with a machine requiring operator assistance. Conversely, the operator is idle when all of the machines are operating without assistance. Operator-machine analysis determines when and how such idle time occurs and helps point out ways to eliminate this wasted time. Specifically, operator-machine analysis studies

1. How to increase the production yield (using the current number of machines)
2. How to calculate the optimal number of machines per operator (such as by ensuring an even distribution of work among operators, increasing the number of machines and/or decreasing the number of operators when possible)
3. How to maintain the current production yield while using fewer machines

Naturally, in studying the operations performed by people or machines, one of the main concerns is to eliminate inefficient use of time, as earlier chapters described regarding operator process analysis. At the same time, remember to carefully consider the equipment layout and the positions of the operators in the workshop as another area in which improvements can reduce the net operating time and eliminate idle time.

Steps in Operator-machine Analysis

As in operator process analysis, the first step is to do a preliminary study of a one-operation cycle, looking at the tasks performed by the operator and, in this case, the operating conditions of the machines. This will give a basic understanding of how the people and the machines are working. Next, enter the measurements onto an operator-machine chart; like the charts previously described, this will help you to plan improvements.

The following is a step-by-step description of a case study in operator-machine analysis. Worker A operates two machines

(1 and 2), but both machines require a lot of assistance. This means that each machine has idle time while worker A is busy assisting the other machine. The example shows how to study the operations of worker A and the two machines with a view toward reducing the machines' idle time and raising their capacity utilization rate.

Step 1: Conduct a preliminary study

At this step, go to the target workshop to ask around, observe, and read up on its production conditions, equipment conditions, layout, process flow, and other factors. Pay especially close attention to the work being done by operators and machines. You may find it helpful to carry out an operator process analysis on the spot, drawing up a process chart to get a better understanding of the workshop's operations.

You should also find out how proficient each operator is, which machines perform what kind of special functions, and any other information that may help you identify problems in the workshop.

Your goals must be specific. You should meet with the workshop supervisor to get advice on what kind of improvement is most needed, whether it be higher efficiency, more machines per operator, fewer machines per operator, or whatever. Once you know what kind of improvement to make, set a precise quantitative goal instead of a vague qualitative one.

In this case study, the goal is to reduce machine idle time and raise the capacity utilization rate.

Step 2: Analyze one operation cycle

At this step, you will carry out separate operator process analyses for each operator or machine that performs operations in one operation cycle. Then you will draw up a flow chart to illustrate these operations. Figure 6-1 shows what the flow chart might look like for this case study.

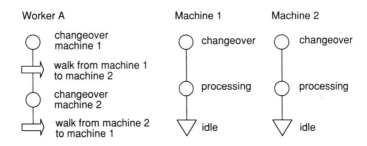

Figure 6-1. Flow Charts

Step 3: Arrange the timing

After making the flow chart, study how the operator and machines work together. Draw horizontal lines on the chart to show when work is being done simultaneously by the operator and one or more of the machines. Figure 6-2 shows how the new flow chart might appear.

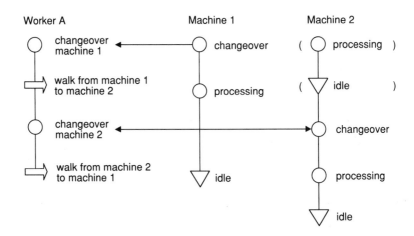

Figure 6-2. Joint Flow Chart Showing Operation Timing

Step 4: Measure the time at each operation step

Next, measure how much time is required for each step observed in step 3. The point is to arrange the timing so that the simultaneous operations match up properly.

Step 5: Draw up an operator-machine chart

In the operator-machine chart, you will use the joint process chart symbols to describe the various steps in the operation cycle. Use the y-axis for time so that longer times produce taller columns in the figure. This will make the arrangement of operation timing clearly visible. Figure 6-3 shows an operator-machine chart for this case study.

Step 6: Organize the analysis results

Table 6-2 shows the data chart for organizing the results of your operator-machine analysis.

Step 7: Work out an improvement plan

Make a list of improvement concerns, such as those shown in Table 6-3, to refer to as you work out an improvement plan based on the operator-machine analysis.

As you can see from the data chart (Table 6-2), in this case worker A is kept quite busy, while both machines (and especially machine 1) have a lot of idle time. In addition, both machines (and especially machine 2) require a lot of operator assistance.

Looking into the reasons for this difference, you find that by changing part of the changeover procedure you can virtually equalize the changeover times for the two machines. You then draw up a new operator-machine chart to reflect this improvement plan (Figure 6-4).

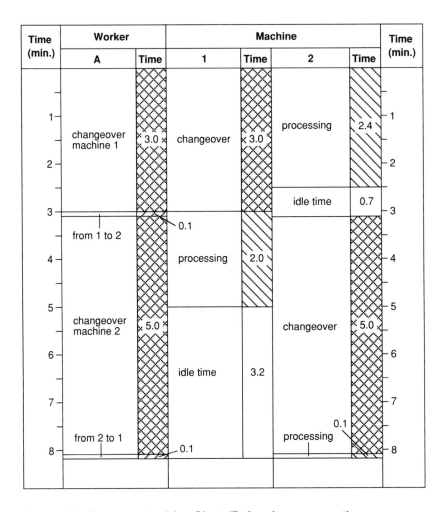

Figure 6-3. Operator-machine Chart (Before Improvement)

Table 6-4 shows a comparison of the operation before improvement and predicted results after improvement. This improvement is estimated to result in a shortening of the total time (i.e., during one operation cycle) from 8.2 minutes to 6.2 minutes and an adjustment in machine 1's idle time percentage

Table 6-2. Data Chart for Operator-machine Analysis

	Worker A		Machine 1		Machine 2	
	Time (min.)	%	Time (min.)	%	Time (min.)	%
Solitary / Automatic	0.2	2	2.0	24	2.5	30
Assisted	8.0	98	3.0	37	5.0	61
Standby / Idle time	0	0	3.2	39	0.7	9
Total	8.2	100	8.2	100	8.2	100

Table 6-3. Improvement Ideas Based on Operator-machine Analysis Results

Analysis Result	Improvement Ideas
1. Operator standby time	• Solve by shortening automatic operation time, accelerating machine operation, improving machine, etc. • Solve by changing assistance time — can operator assistance be done during automatic operation?
2. Machine idle time	• Shorten the operator's solitary operation time • Change the assistance time (such as by automating to eliminate the need for assistance)
3. Operator standby time combined with machine idle time	• Rearrange the sequence of operations • Consider the improvement concerns listed above
4. Very little operator standby time or machine idle time	• Work on improving the work done by the operator and machines

from 39 percent to 19 percent and in machine 2's idle time percentage from 9 percent to 11 percent. The improvement would raise machine 1's capacity utilization rate from 24 percent to 33 percent and machine 2's capacity utilization rate from 30 percent to 41 percent. The production yield would also jump 32 percent $((8.2 \div 6.2) \times 100) =$ approx. 132).

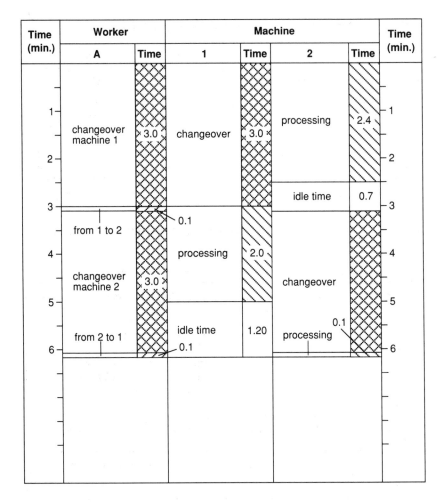

Figure 6-4. Operator-machine Chart (Improvement Plan)

Step 8: Implement and evaluate the improvement plan

Encouraged by these positive estimates, you proceed to implement your improvement and then evaluate it. In your evaluation, you find that although the improvement was successful in that it reduced the operation cycle time by two minutes and boosted production yield more than 30 percent, it left a

Table 6-4. Comparison of Operator-machine Analysis Results with Planned Improvement

	Worker A		Machine 1		Machine 2	
	Before Improve-ment	After Improve-ment	Before Improve-ment	After Improve-ment	Before Improve-ment	After Improve-ment
Solitary / Automatic	0.2 (2)	0.2 (3)	2.0 (24)	2.0 (33)	2.5 (30)	2.5 (41)
Assisted	8.0 (98)	6.0 (97)	3.0 (37)	3.0 (48)	5.0 (61)	3.0 (48)
Standby / Idle time	0 (0)	0 (0)	3.2 (39)	1.2 (19)	0.7 (9)	0.7 (11)
Total	8.2 (100)	6.2 (100)	8.2 (100)	6.2 (100)	8.2 (100)	6.2 (100)

Note: The time unit is minutes; figures in parentheses indicate the percentage of total operation time.

considerable amount of machine idle time and changeover time — points that warrant further improvement efforts.

Step 9: Standardize the improvement

Now that you have confirmed the positive results of your improvement, standardize the new arrangement to prevent backsliding. No improvement plan is perfect — there is always room for further improvement via follow-up measures.

JOINT OPERATION ANALYSIS

What Is Joint Operation Analysis?

Joint operation analysis is the study of the time-based inter-relationship among several operators who perform some type of work together, with the objective of eliminating the Big 3 problems as they exist in this interrelationship. The joint operation chart used for this analysis is similar to the chart used for operator-machine analysis.

In joint operation analysis, you study things such as

1. Standby experienced by each operator
2. Labor capacity utilization of each operator
3. Which of their joint tasks takes the longest

The aim is to achieve results such as

a. Improvement in workload distribution to eliminate standby time in operations
b. Optimal personnel assignments
c. Improvement in the longest task to shorten the total operation time

Steps in Joint Operation Analysis

The steps in joint operation analysis are the same as those in operator-machine analysis. You first carry out an operator process analysis for each operator, then use the results of these analyses to study the timing of their joint operations and find a more efficient arrangement for them. You then draw up a joint operation chart for reference when working out an improvement plan.

The following is a step-by-step description of a case study in joint operation analysis; the operation involves loading a product onto a truck via a sling crane. The operation is done jointly by four workers: two sling loaders (workers A and B), one sling unloader (worker C), and one crane operator (worker D). These workers all have a lot of standby time; therefore the improvement should be aimed at working out a more efficient arrangement of joint operations.

Step 1: Conduct a preliminary study

As in the previous case study, go to the target worksite to ask around, observe, and read up on its production conditions, equipment conditions, layout, process flow, and other factors.

Pay especially close attention to the flow of operations being jointly done by the operators. You should meet with the workshop supervisor to get advice on what kind of specific goal to pursue, such as raising efficiency or reducing labor needs. In this case, the goal is to increase work efficiency.

Step 2: Analyze one operation cycle

Carry out an operator process analysis for each operator in the operation cycle and draw up a flow chart to illustrate these operations. Figure 6-5 shows what the flow chart might look like.

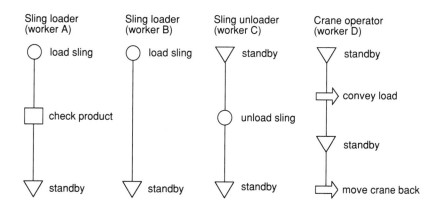

Figure 6-5. Flow Chart

Step 3: Study the timing

Observe which operations are done simultaneously by which operators and draw horizontal lines on the flow chart (Figure 6-5) to show these temporal relationships. Figure 6-6 shows what the new flow chart looks like. Note that the crane operator (worker D) now appears between the sling unloader (worker C) and the sling loader (worker B) to make their joint operations easier to see.

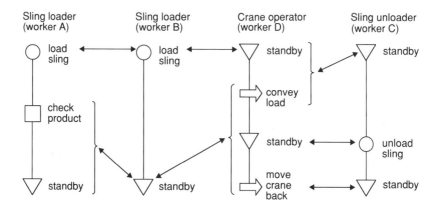

Figure 6-6. Flow Chart Showing Operation Timing

Step 4: Measure the time at each operation step

Now measure how much time is required for each step that you observed in step 3. The point is to arrange the timing so that the simultaneous operations match up properly.

Step 5: Draw up a joint operation chart

The joint operation chart uses joint process chart symbols to describe the various steps in the operation cycle. It has a time-based y-axis so that longer times produce taller columns in the figure, making the arrangement of operation timing clearly visible. Figure 6-7 shows a joint operation chart for this case study.

Step 6: Organize the analysis results

Table 6-5 shows the data chart organizing the results of your joint operation analysis.

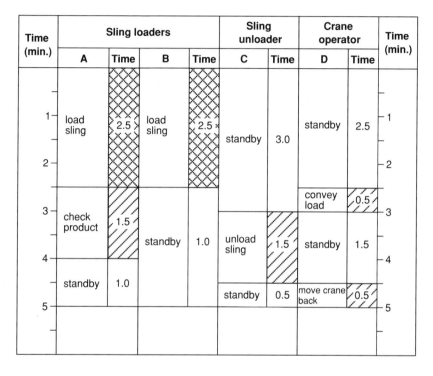

Figure 6-7. Joint Operation Chart (Before Improvement)

Table 6-5. Data Chart for Joint Operation Analysis

	Worker A (sling loader)		Worker B (sling loader)		Worker C (sling unloader)		Worker D (crane operator)		Total	
	Time (min.)	%	Time (min.)	%	Time (min.)	%	Time (min.)	%	Time (min.)	%
Solitary	1.5	30	0	0	1.5	30	1.0	20	4.0	20
Joint	2.5	50	2.5	50	0	0	0	0	5.0	25
Standby	1.0	20	2.5	50	3.5	70	4.0	80	11.0	55
Total	5.0	100	5.0	100	5.0	100	5.0	100	20.0	100

Step 7: Work out an improvement plan

Make a list of improvement concerns (Table 6-6) to refer to as you work out an improvement plan based on your joint operation analysis. As Table 6-5 shows, in this case study the total standby time among the four workers adds up to 55 percent of the total operation time, which may prompt you to ask whether the number of workers can be reduced. The sling unloader (worker C) spends 70 percent of the operation time on standby, and the crane operator is on standby 80 percent of the time.

Table 6-6. Improvement Ideas Based on Joint Operation Analysis Results

Analysis Result	Improvement Ideas
1. Workers who have too much standby time	1. Can the number of workers be reduced? • Can the distribution of work be changed? 2. Can the total required time be shortened? • Change the work sequence • Check into parallel work arrangements
2. Some workers have more standby time than others	1. Reduce standby time for workers who have the most • Shift the workload around to equalize standby time 2. Give first priority to improving operations done by workers who have the greatest workloads
3. Workers who have very little standby time	1. Find ways to improve their operations • Use process analysis or motion study

Noting that workers B and C both are on standby whenever the crane is operated, you come up with the idea of having one of them operate the crane via a wireless remote control box. This makes worker D's role unnecessary for this process. You determine that worker B, who plays only a supportive role in sling loading, should be the one to operate the crane via remote control. You decide not to use worker C for this since his position on top of the truck would make the crane operation task too difficult. You test another idea later on by having the truck driver take over worker C's position.

Figure 6-8 shows the new joint operation chart reflecting your improvement plan. Table 6-7 shows a comparison of the conditions before the improvement and the predicted conditions according to the improvement plan.

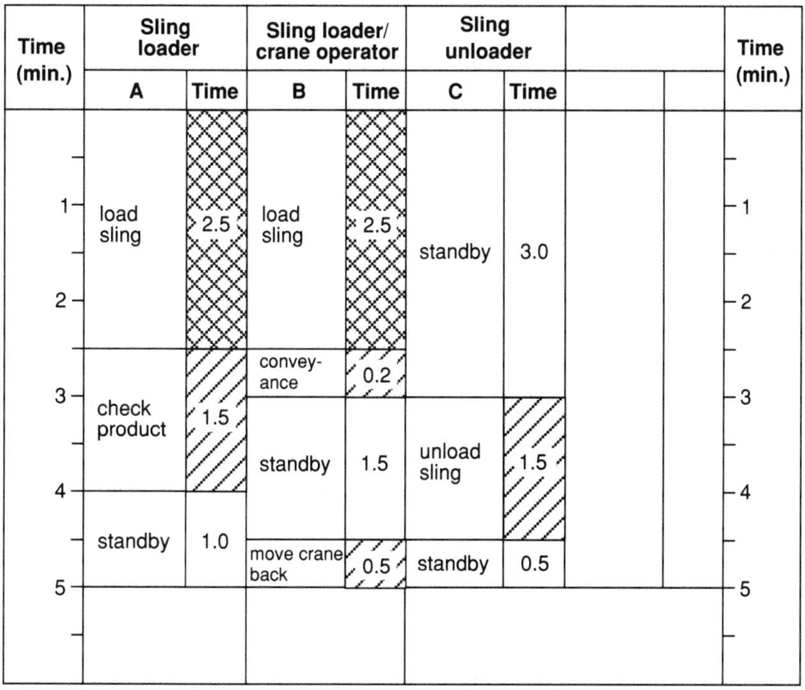

Time (min.)	Sling loader		Sling loader/ crane operator		Sling unloader				Time (min.)
	A	Time	B	Time	C	Time			
1 — 2 —	load sling	2.5	load sling	2.5	standby	3.0			— 1 — 2
3 —	check product	1.5	convey-ance	0.2					— 3
4 —			standby	1.5	unload sling	1.5			— 4
5 —	standby	1.0	move crane back	0.5	standby	0.5			— 5

Figure 6-8. Joint Operation Chart (Improvement Plan)

You have eliminated the need for one of the workers by using a wireless remote control device to operate the crane. However, as Table 6-7 shows, the six minutes of total standby time after the improvement is still excessive (especially for worker C) and warrants further improvement.

Table 6-7. Comparison of Joint Operation Analysis Results (Before Improvement and According to Improvement Plan)

		Worker A (sling loader)		Worker B (sling loader)		Worker C (sling unloader)		Worker D (crane operator)		Total	
		Time (min.)	%	Time (min.)	%	Time (min.)	%	Time (min.)	%	Time (min.)	%
Solitary	Before Improvement	1.5	30	0	0	1.5	30	1.0	20	4.0	20
	Improvement Plan	1.5	30	1.0	20	1.5	30	—	—	4.0	27
Joint	Before Improvement	2.5	50	2.5	50	0	0	0	0	5.0	25
	Improvement Plan	2.5	50	2.5	50	0	0	—	—	5.0	33
Standby	Before Improvement	1.0	20	2.5	50	3.5	70	4.0	80	11.0	55
	Improvement Plan	1.0	20	1.5	30	3.5	70	—	—	6.0	40
Total	Before Improvement	5.0	100	5.0	100	5.0	100	5.0	100	20.0	100
	Improvement Plan	5.0	100	5.0	100	5.0	100	—	—	15.0	100

Step 8: Implement and evaluate the improvement plan

The positive predicted effects of the improvement plan prompt you to go ahead with the plan's implementation and evaluation. To summarize, your improvement in this case reduced the number of workers required by having one of the sling loaders take on the crane operator's job. Naturally, this requires a worker who is qualified to handle both types of jobs.

It also requires a great deal of preparation in establishing proficiency and ensuring safety in remote-control crane operation.

Step 9: Standardize the improvement

Having confirmed the positive results of your improvement, standardize the new arrangement to prevent backsliding. Again, no improvement plan is perfect, and there is always room for improvement through follow-up.

7

Clerical Process Analysis

WHAT IS CLERICAL PROCESS ANALYSIS?

In clerical processing, getting work done is not simply a matter of carrying out a series of operations; you must deal with information in various ways before and after the clerical processing. For instance, clerical workers often have to receive work instructions before they can begin the clerical processing. After they are done, they must check the results, organize the result data, and file a report.

Even in manufacturing companies, a wide variety of clerical processes must be performed, such as

- inspection recordkeeping
- processing of receipts and payments for materials, semifinished products, and products
- recordkeeping concerning breakdowns, accident reports, processing records, statistics, and miscellaneous reports
- updating of employee work records

Naturally, all of these clerical processes consume a lot of time and expense. In general, clerical processes in support of factory operations such as maintenance, warehousing, transportation, and production tend to require even more time and expense than do the operations they support. This is increasingly so in factory automation, in which factory workers are fewer in number and operate mostly as supervisors and maintenance personnel for the automated equipment.

There is no denying that blue-collar work is giving way to white-collar work. But though computers are gradually automating clerical work, this is not always a step forward. Offices that put off computerization until current processes have been thoroughly studied and effective improvement projects have been completed often find that there is no need to computerize. Once the computers have been brought in, on the other hand, making improvements in clerical processes becomes much more complicated.

Clerical processes consist mainly of people, office equipment, and records (information). The type of process analysis to use for clerical work depends on the target of analysis, which is generally either people, combinations of people and machines, or the flow of records (information).

If the target is people, you use operator process analysis. If it is a combination of people and machines, use joint process analysis. If it is the flow of records, use product process analysis. Previous chapters have already shown how to conduct these three types of analysis. The type most commonly used for analyzing clerical processes is product process analysis.

Clerical process analysis is typically understood to mean the study and improvement of recordkeeping and information processing. Obviously, this kind of processing also includes human actions and a certain amount of machine work; when these other types of work play prominent roles in the clerical processes, use operator process analysis and/or joint process analysis to study and improve them.

The process chart symbols for clerical process analysis are almost the same as those used for product process analysis,

Table 7-1. Clerical Process Chart Symbols

Step		Chart Symbol	Description	Comments
Operation		○	Indicates any activity that changes one or more records • Writing • Printing • Filing (bundling, binding, etc.) • Packing	
Transportation		○	Indicates any activity that moves records from one place to another • Moved by people • Moved by machine	The circle for indicating transportation should be one-third to one-half the size of the one used to indicate operations. The arrow symbol can be used instead.
Retention	Storage	▽	Indicates any activity that retains records as scheduled • Storage in warehouses or storerooms • Storage prior to use • Storage after use	
	Delay	D	Indicates any activity that delays records in violation of the schedule • Delay due to operation standbys • Delay due to transportation standbys • Delay due to inspection standbys	
Inspection	Volume inspection	□	Indicates any activity that inspects the number of records	
	Quality inspection	◇	Indicates any activity that inspects the contents of records • Cross-checking, proofing, etc.	
Special symbols	Hand-copying	○◎	Indicates checking two records and hand-copying data from one to another	
	Referring	◇◇	Indicates comparing and checking two records	
	Phone call	○-◎	Indicates writing a phone message in the log	
	Batch convey-ance	⸸	Indicates moving two or more records as one batch	

except that clerical process analysis uses some special symbols to indicate certain types of activities. Table 7-1 lists and describes the various symbols used.

THE PURPOSE OF CLERICAL PROCESS ANALYSIS

Clerical operations are an important part of any manufacturing company, but they do not add value to the company's products. Therefore, the less time and expense such clerical operations require, the better.

However, mistakes in clerical operations can indeed subtract from the value of the company's products and can eventually ruin the company's reputation. An error in transferring information can lead to mistakes in manufacturing operations or in materials supply operations, which can result in big losses for the company.

Information transfer is just one goal of clerical operations, and such operations often involve numerous workshops, offices, and people. During clerical process analysis, it is often essential to gain the cooperation of quite a few people.

In this light, you can begin to understand the primary importance of performing clerical operations correctly. You need to give full consideration to error prevention.

Timing is the second-highest priority. People should receive the information they need, right when they need it.

The third most important thing is to ensure that the information being provided is complete enough and that the information flow is not clogged up with useless data.

Fourth is the need to eliminate inefficiency and waste. This means eliminating the Big 3 problems from clerical operations. The correctness and proper timing of information is much easier to maintain when clerical processes are free of redundant or otherwise unnecessary contents and procedures. Although fourth on our list, this point is nevertheless very important.

The goals of clerical process analysis start with the following:

1. *Standardized operations.* After carefully analyzing and improving a clerical process and clarifying the improvement to all persons concerned, you need to standardize the improved clerical process in a way that is easy for everyone to understand — for example, in a well-written operation manual — to prevent errors and backsliding.

2. *Computerization.* Automation should always be considered as another path to clerical process improvement. Advances in computers and telecommunications equipment can save a lot of time and expense in certain types of clerical operations. Such labor-saving devices include *andon* display lights to show the shop floor situation, other types of display boards, semi-automatic data entry, and automatic input systems. Computers can be a big help for compiling data and generating diagrams.

3. *Elimination of unnecessary recordkeeping.* Perhaps the most important step in clerical process improvement is a critical review of the company's traditional record-keeping methods. Quite often, a company continues to create and process certain types of records even after they have become obsolete. Study each type of record that gets created and processed to determine whether it is really necessary.

    If a record cannot be eliminated, ask whether it can be simplified, combined with another record, or reduced in number. When studying reports, for example, find out whether daily reports are really needed on a daily basis. Perhaps they could serve just as well if issued weekly or even monthly.

To summarize, here is a brief checklist of questions to ask when carrying out a clerical process analysis:

1. Are there any unnecessary records or other information?

2. Is the information that is provided the right kind of information, in the right amount, and going to the right place at the right time?
3. Does it take too long to create records?
4. Can the quantity of records be reduced and/or the contents abbreviated?
5. Are there too many trips involved in moving records? Does it take too long to move the records?
6. Are there any problems in the transportation methods?

To discover better clerical processing methods, you should also study these elements:

- The creation of records and the flow of information (goals: simplification, acceleration, improved accuracy)
- The distribution of work in creating records and processing information
- Possibilities for minimization and simplification of records

STEPS IN CLERICAL PROCESS ANALYSIS

The steps in clerical process analysis are almost the same as those in process improvement and product process analysis, described in earlier chapters. The main difference is that clerical process analysis focuses on using the clerical process chart to study the flow of clerical work and make improvements.

We will look at a step-by-step example of clerical process analysis. At this company, the clerical processes for receiving goods ordered from other companies involve a wide range of employees, such as warehouse workers, buyers, inspectors, and accounting staff. These clerical operations are very time-consuming; in particular, they include some record transfer (hand-copying) work that is in obvious need of streamlining. Imagine that your improvement group has begun to study this situation.

Step 1: Conduct a Preliminary Study

As mentioned in earlier descriptions of process improvements, in this step you must first clarify the problems. Once you have decided on a target for your analysis, make a preliminary study of the target before carrying out the actual analysis. You should ask around, observe, and read up on the following items to get an accurate grasp of the current conditions:

- Records: types, contents, frequency of use, and quantity
- Departments and people involved in the clerical processes
- Flow of records and other information, transportation methods, and time requirements
- Record-creation methods and time requirements
- Relation between clerical processes and items being processed

In this example, where the clerical processes are centered on receiving ordered goods, keep in mind both the flow of records and the flow of received goods as you collect samples of records and study the work done by related people in the warehousing, purchasing, inspection, and accounting departments. In this case, your study reveals the following process-flow conditions:

1. The company that received the order attaches delivery slips and receipts to the ordered goods and delivers them to its warehouse workers.
2. The supplier company's warehouse workers give the received goods a volume inspection, stamp the receipts, and then ship the goods to the factory that ordered them, where they are handed over to the acceptance inspection staff.
3. A purchasing worker at the buyer company prepares a triplicate set of inspection slips based on the delivery slips and sends the inspection slips to the inspection staff via the warehouse staff.

4. Once the inspectors receive the inspection slips, they inspect the goods that were received and put them in temporary storage; then they send the goods, along with two of the inspection slip copies, to the warehouse workers. The other inspection slip copy goes to the accounting staff.
5. Warehouse workers store the goods in the warehouse, then enter the information from the inspection slips into the materials receipts and payments ledger. They keep one of the two inspection slips and send the other one to the purchasing staff for filing.
6. Meanwhile, the accounting employees enter the information from the inspection slip they received into their accounts payable ledger.

Step 2: Create a Clerical Process Chart

Using the process chart symbols shown in Table 7-1, you can now create a clerical process chart showing the flow of goods and records revealed by the preliminary study. In this chart, be sure to include the names of the people and records involved, how the people relate to the flow of goods and/or records, how records relate to each other (as addenda, source information for hand-copying information onto other records, reference information, etc.). The chart should show these items as clearly as possible.

Figure 7-1 shows an example of a clerical process chart for this case study. Although it is simply divided into vertical columns based on the departments involved in the clerical processes, you might also consider adding rows to show time units in a grid, as shown in Table 7-2.

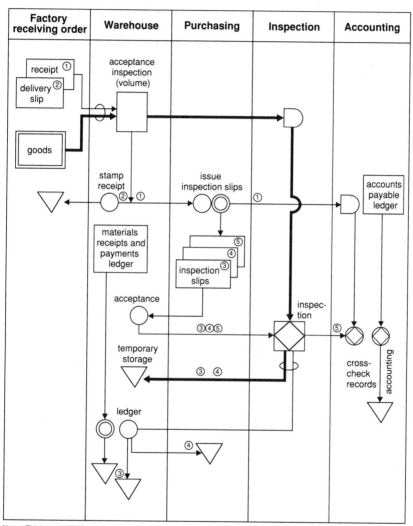

Note: Thick arrows indicate the flow of goods and thin arrows indicate the flow of records.

Figure 7-1. Clerical Process Chart: Acceptance Processes for Ordered Goods (Before Improvement)

Table 7-2. Modified Chart Using Time Units

Time \ Dept.	Factory receiving order	Warehouse staff	- - - - - - - - -
Day 1			
Day 2			
⋮			

Step 3: Draft an Improvement Plan

You are now ready to start considering improvement plan proposals based on the following improvement ideas from examining the clerical process chart (Figure 7-1):

1. Is each type of record really necessary? Can the records' contents or quantity be reduced or otherwise improved?
2. Does generating these records take too much time and trouble? Are there too many occasions when the information on the records needs to be cross-checked or copied over to another record?
3. Is the flow of records smooth or are there trouble spots?
4. Is there room for improvement in the record transport methods?
5. Does the timing of these clerical processes work well with the operation timing of the factory receiving the goods?

At this point, it is good to get advice from the people involved in these clerical processes and to get them involved in small-group activities to help work out the improvement plan. A brainstorming session regarding these clerical processes identifies the following problems:

• It is not necessary for the purchasing staff to prepare a triplicate set of inspection slips based on the delivery

slips. Since it is unnecessary, this process poses an unneeded risk of errors in hand-copying information.
- It is a waste of time for inspection staff to have to wait for the inspection slips to arrive before they can inspect the received goods.

After studying these problems, you decide that it is better if the set of inspection slips is prepared in advance and attached to the delivery slip. The one problem with this proposal is that the delivery slips currently used belong to the supplier company and are designed for their recordkeeping system rather than yours. As a solution to this problem, you decide to design your own four-sheet set of slips (one delivery slip and three copies of the inspection slip) to suit your recordkeeping needs. Your company will supply these to the supplier company when you order goods from them.

This plan eliminates the need for your purchasing staff to fill out any inspection slips and also shortens the delay time for the inspectors who must receive the inspection slips before making their inspections. It also prevents your accounting staff from receiving delivery slips for goods that have not yet been inspected, an improvement that simplifies the cross-checking process. Figure 7-2 shows a clerical process chart of the planned improvement in the flow of records and goods.

Step 4: Implement and Evaluate the Improvement Plan

It is not unusual for clerical processes to involve this many people. When you attempt to improve these processes, remember to first gain the cooperation and support of everyone who will be affected by the improvement. It is good to hold a meeting or training program to help everyone fully understand what the improvement means and how they can help make it work.

The flow of clerical work continues day in and day out, so you must always deal with the problem of how to switch over to the new methods. You need to carefully plan the timing of

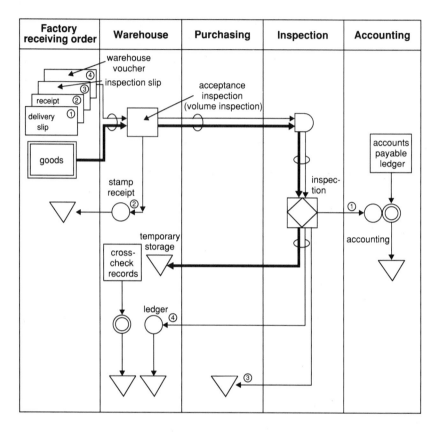

Figure 7-2. Clerical Process Chart: Acceptance Processes for Ordered Goods (Improvement Plan)

this switchover and determine exactly which goods and records will be affected. Naturally, it is essential for all the people who are involved in the flow of records and goods to be involved also in working out the implementation of the improvement plan.

After you have implemented the improvement plan, evaluate the implementation process and determine whether the predicted improvement effects were achieved. For instance, check to see whether the number of records was actually reduced as planned, whether the time required by the clerical processes was shortened, and whether the plan resulted in less or more work for the people involved.

You should also check with the various people and departments concerned to see if any new problems have arisen as a result of the improvement. Do not be surprised to find that such problems have indeed arisen. The thing to do in such cases is simply to follow up with further improvements to eliminate the new problems.

Step 5: Standardize the Improvement

Clerical processes are especially prone to backsliding on recent improvements. Therefore, you need to a make a special effort to carefully plan the standardization of the improvement and to provide instruction booklets and other standardization aids even as you are implementing the improvement. Also be sure to provide any training that is needed to help the new clerical processing methods work smoothly.

Clerical processes are changing rapidly in this era of office automation. This is all the more reason to critically review your clerical processes and discover where there is still room for improvement.

CASE STUDY OF CLERICAL PROCESS ANALYSIS

This case study of clerical process analysis concerns an improvement made by company N in its product shipping operations. Company N produces large volumes of certain parts and sells stock from its warehouse according to orders received. Recently, business competition has grown stronger, pressuring the company to shorten its lead time between receiving orders and shipping products. Company N has also come to recognize improvement of its shipping operations as an important step in raising the company's overall efficiency.

This situation serves as the backdrop for joint improvement activities by two employee groups, one made up of people from the order fulfillment department and the other composed of warehouse staff. Together, these two groups (hereafter called group A and group B, respectively) worked to improve the company's product shipping system.

CASE STUDY

Improvement of Product Shipping Operations at Company N

Formation of a Joint Improvement Group

In the past, each of these improvement groups has worked on various improvement themes related to product shipping operations. Since the improvement theme in this case study deals with several problems that concern both groups, the leader of group B suggested that group A join them in a project aimed at improving the shipping operations. While studying the situation, the joint improvement group also decided to enlist the cooperation of some people in sales-related departments.

Selection of Improvement Theme

To accelerate the product shipment process, the group decided to improve the shipping operations — in particular, the related clerical processes.

Preliminary Study

The preliminary study was split up among the group members so that some people studied the order-reception process, some studied intermediate processes, and some studied the shipment and delivery processes. They paid particular attention to the following:

1. Records: types, contents, frequency of use, quantity, and purpose
2. Types of work done by people involved, and time required
3. Flow of records and other information, conveyance methods and time requirements
4. Record-creation methods (hand-copying, photocopying, cross-checking data) and time requirements
5. Relation between clerical processes and items being processed

Clerical Process Chart (Before Improvement)

Using the results of their preliminary study, the joint group created the clerical process chart shown in Figure 7-3. As the chart shows, when the company receives an order from a client, the sales department gets the order and fills out the order forms on day 1. On day 2, the sales department issues two order vouchers, sending one to the order fulfillment department while the other gets entered into the orders ledger. When people in fulfillment receive the order voucher, they cross-check the voucher against the product payments and receipts ledger and check the inventory conditions. The next day (day 3), they create a shipping schedule.

Next, they write a memo explaining the shipping schedule. Someone takes the memo and schedule to the warehouse, then writes the shipping instructions on a blackboard. Following the instructions on the blackboard, the warehouse workers pack the products and keep an account of their packing work in the packing log. If all goes well, the products are packed within four days of the client's order date.

Meanwhile, the fulfillment department messenger goes back to the fulfillment department, checks over the order voucher

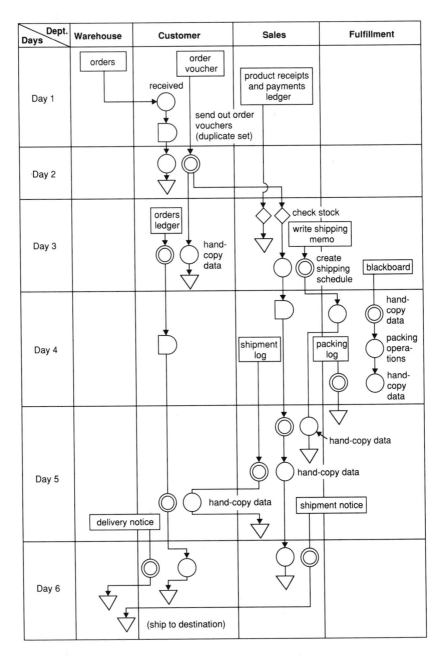

Figure 7-3. Clerical Process Chart: Product Shipping Operations (Before Improvement)

at his or her desk, then enters a description of the shipment in the shipment log. Next, the messenger fills out a shipment notice (postcard) and mails it to the shipping destination (which is not necessarily the client who ordered the product). He or she then hands over the shipment log to the sales department, where someone else enters data such as current date and amount ordered and then fills out a delivery notice and sends it to the client who ordered the product. Normally, the shipment notice and delivery notice both go out on or near day 6, which is two or three days after the products are shipped out.

The joint group discovered the following problems during its preliminary study:

1. Too much time elapses between receiving the order and shipping the product.
2. Too much time elapses between shipping the product and getting out the shipment and delivery notices.
3. There are too many types of records being used (10 types) and too much hand-copying (6 times per order). Too many memos are used when vouchers would be more appropriate.
4. Hand-copying shipping instructions onto a blackboard is troublesome and easily leads to transcription errors.
5. It is illogical that the shipment notice and delivery notice are filled out by different departments.

Drafting an Improvement Plan

After studying the problems listed above and brainstorming with the various group members and other concerned parties, the joint group came up with the following improvement plan:

1. Instead of hand-copying order voucher data onto the order ledger, the company will use loose-leaf file forms for the order vouchers so that the vouchers can be filed to actually become the ledger. The packing log and

shipment ledger will also be replaced by more efficient shipping instruction forms and order vouchers, as described below.

2. Instead of using a blackboard at the warehouse, the fulfillment department staff will fill out a shipment instruction form in duplicate. This form will eliminate the risk of transcription error posed by the blackboard method. One copy of the shipment instruction form will be left at the warehouse to eliminate the need for hand-copying the data into a log. The other copy will be returned to the fulfillment department, which will check to make sure that the products were actually shipped.

3. Since the contents of an order's shipment notice and delivery notice are almost the same, the sales department was assigned the task of photocopying the data from one to the other and mailing both notices.

4. After the above improvements are made, the group reckons that the shipping instruction forms can be issued on day 2, the products shipped on day 3, and the shipment notice and delivery notice mailed on day 4.

Figure 7-4 is a clerical process chart showing the flow of shipping operations according to this improvement plan.

Effects of Improvement

The improvement's effects included the following:

1. First of all, it shortened the shipment lead time. What used to take six days can now be done in four. This faster lead time is very much appreciated by company N's clients.

2. Three types of record books (the orders ledger, packing log, and shipment log) were eliminated along with the shipping memos, and almost all hand-copying also was eliminated.

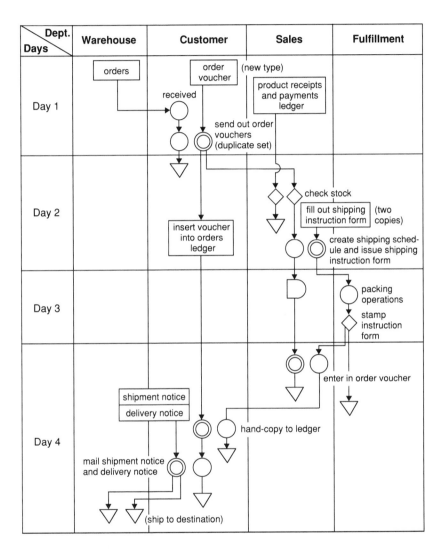

Figure 7-4.   Clerical Process Chart: Product Shipping Operations (Improvement Plan)

3. No one has to copy information onto a blackboard anymore. The shipment instruction forms that are used instead provide a clearer description of the shipment

information, which improves management effectiveness.

4. The method for filling out shipment and delivery notices was improved, and their issue date was moved up.

Implementation and Standardization

Since all of the supervisors and other concerned parties were consulted in advance about this improvement, there was no problem in printing up the new forms and training everyone in the new procedures. After implementing the improvement, the people involved found that they were not only able to keep to the accelerated shipment operations schedule but even had a little time left over.

Some of the people involved in these operations found it hard at first to break the habit of carrying memos around, but they are being trained to use the new vouchers correctly and to avoid using memos.

Company N's customers were pleased with the shorter lead time. The new shipping procedures went smoothly and without any errors. Everyone approved the new schedule and now checks up on it periodically.

Review and Issues for the Future

Although the joint group members found it hard to understand how the clerical processes had been working and were concerned that their improvement efforts might not succeed, they put their heads together and with the help of the clerical process analysis method were able to solve the targeted problems.

These improvement groups now hope to make further improvements in clerical processes. Their confidence boosted by this success, they are now taking on broader organizational problems related to the distribution of work within the company.

8
Process Analysis Case Studies

OVERVIEW

Recently, QC circle activities in Japan have made increasing use of IE methods. This chapter presents three case reports of such uses from *Factory Quality Control (FQC)* magazine; these are summarized below.

Case Study 1: Labor-hour Reduction in Manual Processes through IE Improvement Activities

This case concerns an improvement made in a ceramistor assembly process. The improvement was made by the assembly group in section 3 of the ceramistor department at Hokkaido Matsushita Electric Company.

The leader of this group put the lessons of an in-house IE course he had taken to work by studying IE methods with his group and using these methods in an improvement project. Their goal for this project was to achieve a 10 percent reduction in the labor-hours required for their manual processes (inserting and soldering elements). Using product process analysis and motion study, they were able to exceed their targeted labor-hour reduction.

This case study offers many pointers for other improvement groups. Please apply the lessons of this case study to your own workshop, and see if it helps you find places where there is still room for improvement.

Case Study 2: Shortening Process Stops

This improvement project was carried out by the "Three Aces" circle in section 2 of manufacturing department 1 at Sekisui Chemical's Mizuguchi Plant in Shiga Prefecture, Japan. The improvement goal was to shorten the process stop time from 20 minutes to 10 minutes. The group succeeded in reducing it to just 7 minutes.

This case is a good example of how operator process analysis can be used to discover problems and make corrective improvements. It serves as a good reference for other groups that want to use process analysis to help standardize operations and sharpen their focus on problems to make more effective improvements.

Case Study 3: Improvement of LC Heat Operations

This improvement project was carried out by the "Capsule Heat" circle in section 1 of the production packaging department at Kissei Pharmaceuticals. Circle members improved their process setup procedures and thereby raised their production output. They used joint process analysis and time study to discover how they could reduce the equipment's nonoperating time as part of their improvement.

This case can serve as a good lesson not only in the use of joint process analysis and time study but also in the power of keeping a positive attitude toward making improvements.

We hope that these three case studies will help your own QC group put IE methods to use in making workshop improvements.

CASE STUDY 1

Labor-hour Reduction in Manual Processes through IE Improvement Activities
"The Thrill of Discovery: Finding Waste in Operations"
by Yoshihisa Kato, Hokkaido Matsushita Electric Co.

The members of our group all do different kinds of work, so at first we understood little about each other's jobs. Our QC circle activities have helped us to understand these better and have boosted our team spirit. Our members are very energetic, and we hope to put more of that energy to work in future QC activities.

Background

Our factory manufactures ceramic semiconductors — electronic components that take advantage of the electrical characteristics of ceramic materials. In our workshop, we assemble ceramistors, which are devices that prevent images shown on television tubes from being disturbed by electro-magnetic radiation.

This case report describes an improvement activity in which our group studied and applied IE techniques that I had just learned in an in-house IE training course.

Understanding Current Conditions Prior to Selecting the Improvement Theme

We began by diagraming our process (see Figure 8-1) and drawing up a flow diagram of the product assembly steps contained therein (see Figure 8-2). The first problems that we noticed were the following:

1. The transportation distance was much too long (a total of 408 meters!).
2. The processes are spread out all over the workshop.
3. The workpieces have to be moved around a lot at the insertion and soldering processes.
4. A Pareto diagram to study labor-hour concentrations showed that the element insertion and soldering processes account for as much as 45 percent of total labor-hours.

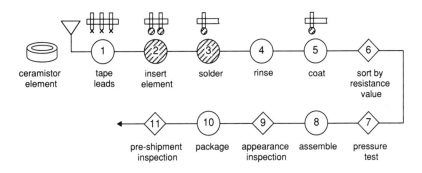

Figure 8-1. Process Outline

We considered that the first two problems would be difficult to address because another team's products are sometimes taken through these processes. We decided that, for the time being, we would attack the problem of excessive labor-hours at the element insertion and soldering processes.

These two processes have an especially important influence on product quality, particularly on its electrical characteristics. At present, most of the work done at these processes is manual work.

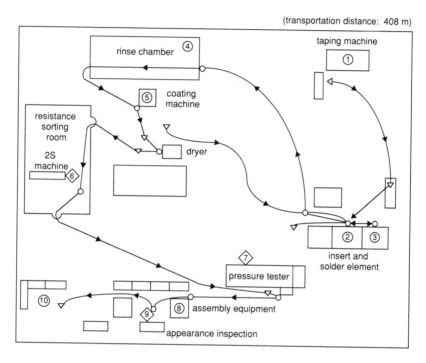

Figure 8-2. Flow Diagram

Working Out a Plan for Improvement Activities

Following the IE activities steps for this improvement theme, we assigned various jobs to group members, giving the biggest jobs to the three of us who actually work in the element insertion and soldering processes (see Table 8-1).

Establishing a Target Value

We decided that our target would be to achieve a 10 percent reduction in the labor-hours (as measured in April) for the element insertion and soldering processes by June.

Table 8-1. Activities Schedule and Job Assignments

Month / Activities	J	F	M	A	M	J	J	Members' jobs
Analyze current conditions	• Flow diagram, process analysis • Pareto chart, therblig analysis ○ ·············· ○							• Naruto • Nakamura
Identify problems	• Identify and summarize ○ ·············· ○							• Ito • Naruto
Study and implement improvement plan					• Propose, test, and carry out plan ○ ········· ○			All members
Check results						• Standardize ○ ··········· ○		All members

Analyzing Current Conditions

Process analysis

After we drew up a process chart of the product flow (see Figure 8-3), we found the following problems:

1. Too much transportation (11 trips) and too many delays (8 times)
2. Processing time is 52 percent of total time and transportation time is 48 percent

Motion study (therblig analysis)

Using therblig analysis,* we broke the operations down into motion units to get a better look at where the problems

---

* Therbligs are symbols for units of motion, developed by Frank Gilbreth as an aid to motion study. See the *Motion Study* volume of this series (Productivity Press, 1991). — Ed.

Date: _____

	(Before Improvement)	Name: Yoshihisa Kato	Checked by: (stamp)	Inspected by: (stamp)	Chart by: (stamp)
Analysis range:	Element insertion and soldering				
Product name:	Ceramistor	Division: Hokkaido (division or plant)			
Analysis target	Check one: __ product __ operator	Dept.: Ceramistor Parts Team: Assembly			

No.	Step	Operation	Transport	Delay	Inspection	Time	Distance (m)	People	No. of units	Equipment, jigs, tools	Materials
1	Move rack from taping machine to counter	○	●	▽	□		20		15,000	rack	
2	Standby at counter	○	○	▼	□						
3	Take wires only to work table	○	●	▽	□		24		9,000		wires
4	Standby at work table	○	○	▼	□						
13	Move pallet to work table	○	●	▽	□		10		9,000		element
14	Standby at work table	○	○	▼	□						
15	Remove paper only from table	○	●	▽	□					cart	
16	Standby	○	○	▼	□						
17	Solder workpiece	●	○	▽	□					solder	
18	Return to pallet	○	●	▽	□	29				soldering	solder
19	Take to cart	○	●	▽	□		90		300		
20	Do same for 30 pallets total	○	○	▼	□			3			
21	Transport to rinsing chamber	○	●	▽	□		20		9,000	cart	

Summary	Time	Distance (m)	People								
				Labor-hours	2	11	8	0			
				Time	52	48	0	0			
	100	408	5	People used	5						

Figure 8-3. Process Chart (Before Improvement)

existed (see Figure 8-4). Since these IE methods were new to me and to the other group members, we asked an IE instructor to help us with the textbooks that we needed to use in making our analysis. This instructor was also kind enough to study the analysis results with us. In going over the analysis results, we discovered the following things:

1. The worker had to hold the wires steady with her fingers so they would not slip around.
2. Quite often, she was not doing anything with her left hand.
3. There were a lot of repeated motions in this operation.
4. There were a lot of motions in which items were simply switched from one hand to the other.

Implementing the Improvement Plan

We held a brainstorming session to come up with improvement ideas for the situation we had observed. Finally, with the cooperation of various other employees, we implemented the following improvement plan.

Improvement to reduce transportation trips at element insertion and soldering processes

Once the inserted elements have been brought to the cart, the soldering worker takes them from the cart and solders them. To improve this method, we decided that once the elements on the cart have been inserted they should be soldered before being returned to the cart; this would reduce the number of transportation trips (see Figure 8-5).

Elimination of wire holding when soldering

Before the improvement, the soldering worker would first set the wires upright into a jig and then would hold each wire as

Date: ______________

	(Before Improvement)	Name: Yoshihisa Kato	Checked by: (stamp)	Inspected by: (stamp)	Chart by: (stamp)
Product name:	**Ceramistor**				
Operation name:	**Element insertion and soldering**	**Division: Hokkaido**			
Operator name:	**Noriko Nakamura**	**Dept.: Ceramistor Parts**	**Team: Assembly**		

No.	Operation Elements	Left-hand Motion	Therbligs Left		Therbligs Right	Right-hand Motion	Improvement Concerns
1	↑	Reach (30 cm) to get wires	◡	↑	◡	Reach to get wires	• Can wires be moved to a better place?
2	│	Grasp wires (in paper rack)	∩	│	∩	Grasp wires (in paper rack)	
3	│	Carry wires	⌓	│	⌓	Carry wires	• Can wire insertions be done any faster?
4	│	Hold wires steady in paper rack (10 times)	∪	│	∩	Hold wires	
5	│	Hold inserted wires	⊓	│	◡	Reach for elements	• Can wires be inserted using both hands?
6	Insert	Hold inserted wires	│	│	∩	Grasp elements	• How many elements are picked up at once? Must this be done 10 times?
7	│	Hold inserted wires	│	│	⌓	Carry back wires	
8	│	Hold inserted wires	↓	│	♀	Insert wires	
9	│	Hold in other hand	∩	│	∩	Hold in other hand	
10	│	Carry back	⌓	│	⌓	Carry back	
11	↓	Put down	⊝	↓	⊝	Put down	
12	↑	Reach for inserted items	◡	↑	◡	Reach for inserted items	
13	│	Pick up inserted items	∩	│	∩	Pick up inserted items	
14	│	Carry back inserted items	⌓	│	⌓	Carry back inserted items	• Can more soldering be done at the same time?
15	│	Put down inserted items	⊝	│	⊝	Put down inserted items	
16	│	Reach for solder	◡	│	◡	Reach for soldering gun	
17	│	Pick up solder	∩	│	∩	Pick up soldering gun	
18	Solder	Carry back solder	⌓	│	⌓	Carry back soldering gun	
19	│	Attach solder	♀	│	♀	Aim soldering gun	10 times
20	│	Pick up soldered items	∩	│	∩	Hold soldering gun	• Can this trip be eliminated?
21	│	Carry back soldered items	⌓	│	│	Carry back soldering gun	
22	│	Put down soldered items	⊝	│	↓	Put down soldering gun	
23	↓	Shift solder to right hand	⊝	↓	∩	Grasp solder	• Can shifting solder to the right be eliminated?

Figure 8-4. Therblig Analysis Chart

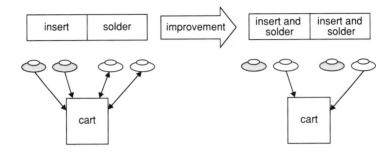

Figure 8-5. Elimination of Transportation Trips

she soldered it to keep it from slipping. We improved this by
having the wires set down on their sides, thereby eliminating the
need to hold each one steady when soldering (see Figure 8-6).

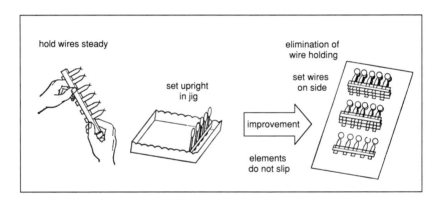

Figure 8-6. Elimination of Wire Holding During Soldering

These two improvements were almost enough to get us to
our targeted labor-hour reduction. However, when we compared the labor-hour requirements for soldering other types of
products, we realized our process was still too labor intensive.
Therefore, we went back to another improvement concern that
was pointed out during our preliminary analysis but never
acted on, namely our soldering technique.

Reduction of soldering labor-hours by use of dip-soldering method

We learned that if this particular product is dip-soldered in the same way that other products are, some flux remains on the element and cannot be rinsed off completely, and the unstable preheating temperature of the dip-soldering method poses a risk that the element will be damaged. We came up with a new method for dip-soldering the elements (see Figure 8-7).

1. Working with the technical staff, we developed a pre-heating jig that keeps the molten solder at an even temperature.
2. After solving the preheating problem, we were able to solder as many as 300 elements at once by dipping them into the solder vat.
3. We measured the flux thickness every day and adjusted it to prevent flux adherence.

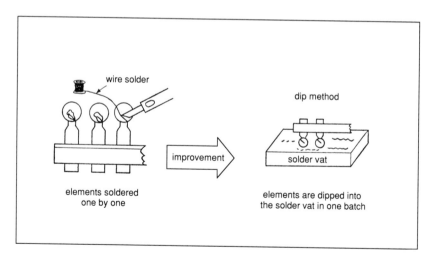

Figure 8-7. Reduction of Labor-hours in Soldering

Checking the Results of Improvement

We confirmed the following results from our improvements:

1. The improvement reduced the number of transportation trips in the element insertion and soldering processes (9,000 elements tested).
   Before improvement: 11 trips
   After improvement: 8 trips
   Transportation time was reduced to 84 percent of the previous total.
2. The improvement eliminated the need to hold the wires steady during soldering.
3. The improvement introduced a new soldering method (dip-soldering).

Figure 8-8 shows the labor-hour reduction achieved by this improvement. As the figure shows, we surpassed our target reduction. The monetary value of this improvement has been calculated as ¥690,000 ($4,600) per month.

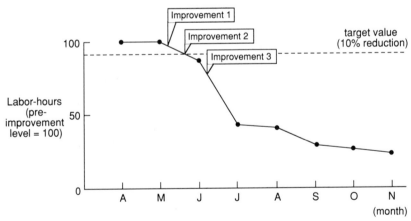

Figure 8-8. Effect of Improvement

Standardizing

We carried out the following standardization measures:

1. We revised the production specifications manual, with the help of the related technical staff.
2. We revised the operator's instruction manual, with the help of the related technical staff.
3. We created a check sheet to use in monitoring the solder preheating temperature and the flux thickness.

Review and Future Issues

This improvement project was a challenge for us because we were trying out some IE methods that we had just learned and some unfamiliar work methods, too. Consequently, we lacked confidence in our understanding of what we were doing. With the help of our IE instructor, however, we were able to achieve very satisfactory results. For the future, we intend to continue studying and using IE methods as we broaden the scope of our activities to include everyone in our workshop.

CASE STUDY 2

Shortening Process Stops
**"IE Brings Success in Improving Continuous Process
Operations at a Chemical Factory"**
by Kenji Higashi, Sekisui Chemicals

Two workshop colleagues and I formed the "Three Aces" circle in April 1977. We all hoped that the circle activities would help us become "ace" employees. At first, we worked mainly on improving some of our company's proprietary technologies, but our efforts were thwarted by a lack of support data and other difficult conditions that put us way behind schedule in our improvement activities.

With the help of some of our managers, we learned new methods, such as how to gather and analyze data before implementing the improvement. Since then we have been able to carry out several successful improvement projects without falling behind schedule. We have learned to bring improvement consciousness into our everyday work and are proud to say that we have become the most advanced improvement group in our department.

Background

Our factory is located in Mizuguchi-machi, a beautiful area in the Koga region of Shiga prefecture. At our workshop, we make a resin that is used as a laminant in safety glass for automobile windshields.

Our factory runs on day and night shifts. On both shifts, we work to improve our workshop by striving to solve whatever problems come to our attention during our work.

Selecting the Improvement Theme

We first listed 16 problems that are considered either too labor-intensive (requiring too many labor-hours) or too difficult (because of environmental factors). We got together to evaluate and prioritize these 16 items so that we could select the most pressing problem as our improvement theme (see Table 8-2 for a partial listing).

Reasons for Selecting Improvement Theme

Process stops are events in which we have to quickly stop the resin-making process to carry out some task.

Table 8-2. Selection of Improvement Theme

Evaluation item / Problem areas	Closeness of problem	Difficult task?	Improvement involving everyone?	Management policy?	Manual work involved?	Improvable within 6 months?	Impact	Overall Rating
Takes too long to wipe out the dryer's supply port	△	△	○	△	△	△	△	5
Too hard to retrieve the resin residue	○	○	○	×	△	△	○	2
Empty bags that contained the material must be organized	○	△	△	×	△	○	×	6
Takes too long to stop the process	○	○	○	○	△	○	○	1 ◎
Neutralizer strainers must be changed	○	○	○	△	△	△	△	3
Takes too long to operate the decanter's thermal	△	○	△	○	△	×	○	4

1. Since we are on a three-shift schedule to keep the line running, only one of us is running the line when a stop must be done, and we would like to keep the downtime to within 10 minutes.
2. The process stop operation covers a wide area that includes three floors in the factory, and it involves the hand-turning of many valves. All this makes for difficult working conditions during the process stop operation.
3. The process operators do not all use identical work procedures, so when each person starts a shift he or she must first check all of the valve positions.

Improvement Schedule

We scheduled our improvement project to begin on April 1 and finish by September 30.

Process Outline

The process includes the following stages:

Dissolving → reaction → rinsing → neutralizing → drying

Studying Current Conditions

First, we studied how often process stop operations were being carried out. Periodic process stop operations were done every eight months. However, after combining such periodic process stops with unplanned emergency stops, we found that the process was stopped an average of five times every month.

When observing how each operator carries out a process stop operation, we found a wide variety of methods being used. We also found quite a few differences in work methods even when comparing the operators' normal daily operations. We then created a survey form to check how many valves were being operated, and also how many valves per floor. We asked another person in our workshop to carry out this survey for us (see Figures 8-9 and 8-10).

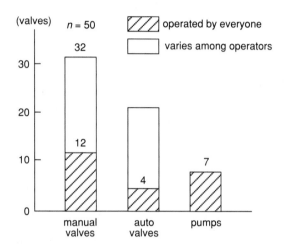

Figure 8-9. Number of Valves (and Pumps) Operated

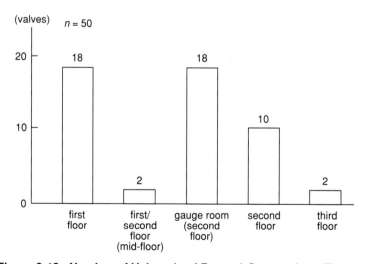

Figure 8-10. Number of Valves (and Pumps) Operated per Floor

The results of this survey showed that 50 valves were being operated in an area covering three floors in the factory, and that the methods for operating these valves varied widely among workers. This led us to wonder if we could use IE techniques to improve our operation methods. We consulted with our managers and began studying how to do a process analysis (see Figure 8-11).

No.	Operations	Flow	Time (sec.)	Distance (meters)	Opera-tions	Trans-portation	Inspec-tion	Standby	Comments
Title: Process Stop Operation									
1		⇨	12	20					
2	gauge room	◯	2						get tools
3		⇨	70	156					
4	3-way valve 3d floor)	◯	58						cut off line
5		⇨	64	150					
46	dispersion vat (2d floor)	◯	8						close water supply valve
47		⇨	42	66					
	Totals			1,052	20 times	23 times	3 times	1 time	
			1,191		490 sec.	582 sec.	38 sec.	81 sec.	

Figure 8-11. Process Chart (Before Improvement)

This analysis revealed just how many transportation trips our process stop operation includes — the operator must walk more than 1,000 meters within a process stop operation that lasts 20 minutes.

Setting an Improvement Target

We set a reduction in the process stop operation time from 20 minutes to 10 minutes as our improvement target.

Drafting an Improvement Plan

We came up with more than four improvement plan proposals based on a set of 25 improvement items. We evaluated these proposals in terms of their implementation cost, estimated effects, and other factors, then selected and implemented the three improvement plans described in Table 8-3 below.

Table 8-3. Description of Improvement Plans

	Problems	Improvement Goal	Operations	Improvement Plan	Predicted Problems
1	Too many pump operations	Eliminate some pump operations	1. Pumps in production line 2. Valve-turning operations	• Get rid of pump operations • Do not close valve on inlet side of pump (keep valve open)	Line blockage Line blockage
2	Too many valve operations	Consolidate valves	1. Water supply to neutralization vat shaft 2. Water supply to pump	• Bring valves together at one place • Bring valves on the second floor together at one place	Water supply valves will get blocked at the start
3	Work area too big (three floors)	Consolidate work area on one floor	1. Switch to circulating line	• Switch to circulating line on the second floor	Stabilize flow rate in circulating line

Implementing Improvements

Improvement 1: To eliminate some of the pump operations while also preventing pump line blockage, we decided to leave open all the valves that had previously been operated each time the pump was used. This improvement eliminates the need to operate all those valves.

Improvement 2: We consolidated some valve operations by moving the water supply valve that was operated on the first floor for the first floor's neutralization vat up to the second floor, so that both vat supply valves could be operated from the second floor.

Improvement 3: We consolidated the work area (see Figures 8-12 and 8-13).

The most troublesome improvement item was the operation controlling water circulation to the neutralization vats. This operation required the worker to go all the way up to the third floor. As shown in part (a) of Figure 8-12, we moved the line and the valve to the second floor so it could be operated there. However, after doing this, we found that we could not maintain the required flow rate.

Next, we tried regulating the flow rate by adding narrow sections to the line as shown in part (b) of Figure 8-12, but this did not work either. Then we tried using a simple flow regulator that had been lying around unused. We attached it to the line as shown in part (c) of Figure 8-13. However, the flow regulator caused overflow problems and could not be used after all.

We reevaluated the situation and finally came up with an idea that worked. We inserted a flow-adjusting stick into the flow regulator to reduce the flow rate to the required level. This enabled us to move the valve operation to the second floor as planned and resulted in a substantial reduction in labor-hours for the process stop operations.

Confirming Improvement Effects

We wrote up a new process chart to describe our improvement plan (see Figure 8-14). Our improvement brought the following results:

1. We eliminated the difference in the number of valves used by each worker.
2. We removed all of the valve operations from the first floor, first/second mid-floor, and third floor, consolidating them in the gauge room on the second floor.
3. We reduced the process stop operation time from 20 minutes to just 7 minutes (exceeding our target of 10 minutes).

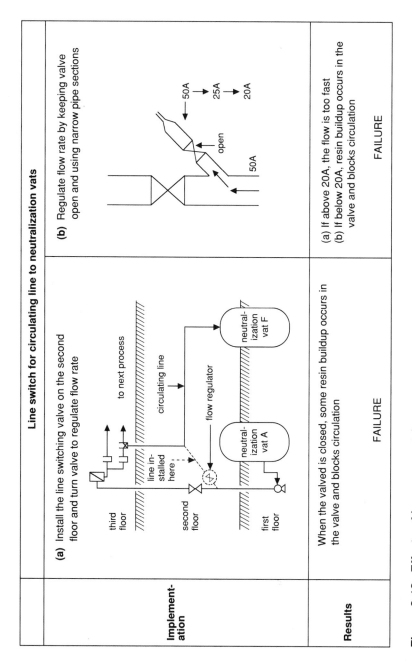

Figure 8-12. Effects of Improvement 1

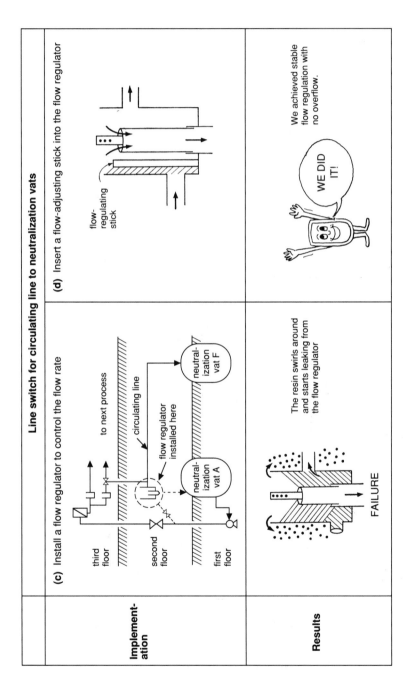

Figure 8-13. Effects of Improvement 2

We also drew a diagram showing the tangible and intangible effects these results represent (see Figure 8-15).

No.	Operations	Flow	Time (sec.)	Distance (meters)	Opera-tions	Trans-portation	Inspec-tion	Standby	Comments
	Title: Process Stop Operation								
1		⇨	4	2		●			
2	gauge room (2d floor)	○	2		●				stop No. 4 pump
3		⇨	34	52		●			
4	neutralization vat F (2d floor)	○	16		●				set flow regulator return line
5		⇨	12	10		●			
21									
22	dispersion vat E (2d floor)	○	8		●				close water supply valve
23		⇨	36	66		●			
	Totals			528	9 times	12 times	2 times	0 times	
			412		300 sec.	300 sec.	10 sec.	0 sec.	

Figure 8-14. Process Chart (After Improvement)

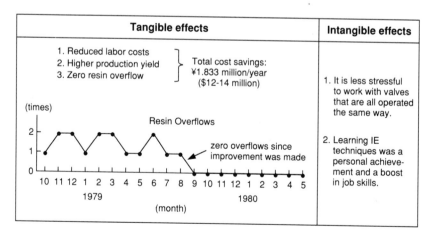

Figure 8-15. Tangible and Intangible Effects

Standardizing

We added a detailed description of the new process stop methods into the operations manual and standardized these methods to eliminate operator-specific differences.

Summary and Plans for the Future

We ran into one dead end after another when attempting to implement the third improvement plan. However, encouraged by our managers and filled with determination, we kept trying out new ideas, putting our many days of study to work. Needless to say, when we finally succeeded, we were left with renewed confidence and optimism about making further improvements in the future. We also gained new strength as a group of three people intent on becoming "aces." We look forward to using our individual wits and collective wisdom in future circle activities.

CASE STUDY 3

Improvement of LC Heat Operations
"Individual Strength, Teamwork, and Study"
by Masaichi Kamijo, Kissei Pharmaceuticals

Our QC circle meets every Wednesday during the lunch hour. We have become a very close-knit group, working hard toward common goals. Our circle includes people of various ages, and we maintain a very warm and friendly atmosphere in which everyone can feel free to speak his or her mind.

We each pull our own weight in this workshop. Some days are fun and other days are a strain, but we are confident of continued success in our circle activities.

Background

We work at Kissei Pharmaceuticals, whose company mottoes are "Serving society with high-quality pharmaceutical products" and "Helping society by helping its members." Our research and sales staff members are constantly striving to provide safer and more effective pharmaceutical products. Through our network of sales offices throughout Japan, we are proud to play a major part in maintaining people's health.

Our workshop is part of the company's packaging operations for capsule, tablet, and powder medicines. Our process handles mostly tablets but also some powders, and we work in day and night shifts.

Reasons for Selecting Improvement Theme

With advice from managers and others, we selected our improvement theme through the process shown in Figure 8-16.

Setting a Target and Selecting Study Items

After it became clear that the LC heat machine's net capacity utilization rate was low, we made a Pareto chart to search for the reasons. The Pareto chart showed us that setup and clean-up accounted for about 70 percent of the machine's downtime (see Figure 8-17). Table 8-4 shows the results of our study of the machine's operation using 210-kilogram lots, in which we paid close attention to these setup and clean-up problems. Table 8-5 shows the improvement goals that we set.

Study Session

Some of our group members became discouraged when they heard that our next step was to analyze the setup and

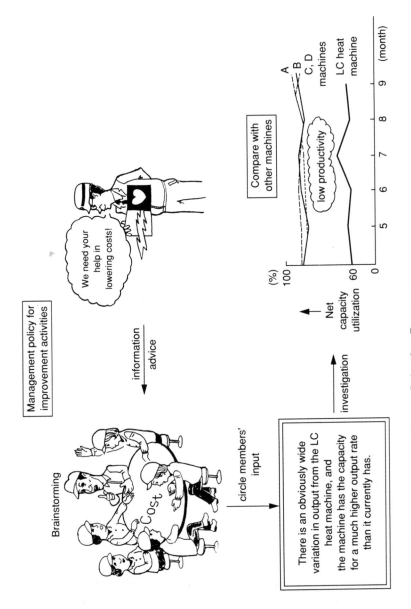

Figure 8-16. Improvement Theme Selection Process

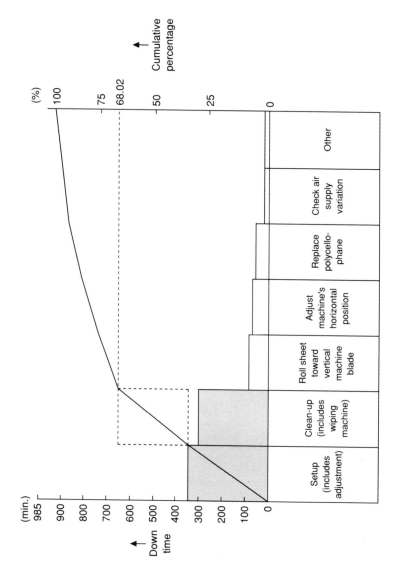

Figure 8-17. Pareto Chart: Reasons for Low Capacity Utilization Rate (Lot Size: 210 kg)

Table 8-4. Study of Production Conditions (210-kg Lots)

Work Days	Output (kg)	Setup time (min.)	Clean-up time (min.)
Day 1	20	200 (includes adjustments)	
2			
3			
4	35	25	30
5			
6			
Last day	15		140 (includes wiping machine)

Table 8-5. Improvement Goals

		Current	Target
Higher output	Day 1	20 kg	35 kg
	Day 2 and after	35 kg	42 kg
Shorter wiping time	Last day	140 min.	70 min.

Project period	3 months

clean-up operations. This is because previously we had used the continuous observation method (a type of time study), in which an observer works one-on-one with an operator to analyze an operation from start to finish. They remembered how tiring that was.

What made that experience particularly exasperating was that we repeatedly made minor omissions in the observation records and had to start over again. This time, we needed to monitor three operators at the same time! That meant we needed to have three observers watching continuously for long periods of time. It sounded impossible.

We were already familiar with the work sampling (operation analysis) and PTS (predetermined time system) methods, but neither of those was appropriate for our current situation. That left us searching for another method. We began checking in bookstores and in the company library, hoping to find a suitable study method. Finally, we found what we needed: "micro time study using a tape recorder."

Although the operations we were going to study were unit operations rather than micro-motion operations, we recognized that this method would still be appropriate for our need to study the motions of three people at once. When our circle members heard the description of the method, they thought that it sounded like fun, like "something we could do." We were all eager to try the new method (see Figure 8-18).

At our next circle meeting, we were ready to learn how to create a report based on our analysis results. Fortunately, our circle leader had just finished studying multiple activity analysis and operator process analysis in the company-sponsored correspondence course. He organized a study session to teach other members what they needed to know to make a results report.

This was not an easy thing for us to learn. Our group consists of various age groups, and many members found it hard to understand how to organize the data and work out improvement plans. For them, the study session turned into a lot of extra work during lunch hours and at home. I do not know whether it was because of our group's informal attitude (our meetings sometimes seem more like tea parties than study sessions) or because the members were so optimistic and enthusiastic, but every one of us finally mastered the new techniques.

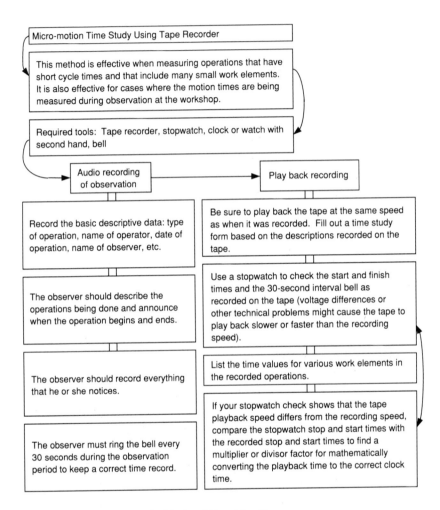

Figure 8-18. Time Study Method Used by Group

Analyzing Current Conditions Using a Tape Recorder

When observing the LC heat operations, we realized that we could not get accurate data if the operator is not used to having someone with a tape recorder observing and recording what is going on. Therefore, we first observed some other operations, and while doing that we developed the observation method shown in Figure 8-19. These "practice" observations got the employees used to being observed and recorded and also gave us some practice in operation analysis.

record book

stop-
watch

microphone

containers

Figure 8-19. Operation Observation Method

We picked three operators of average experience and skill and analyzed all of the setup operations that they perform throughout the several days of the production run (see Figure 8-20).

Analyzing Problems and Drafting Improvement Measures

We drew up a cause-and-effect diagram to better understand the problems in the various setup operations (see Figure 8-21). We then came up with various improvement measures to solve these problems (see Table 8-6).

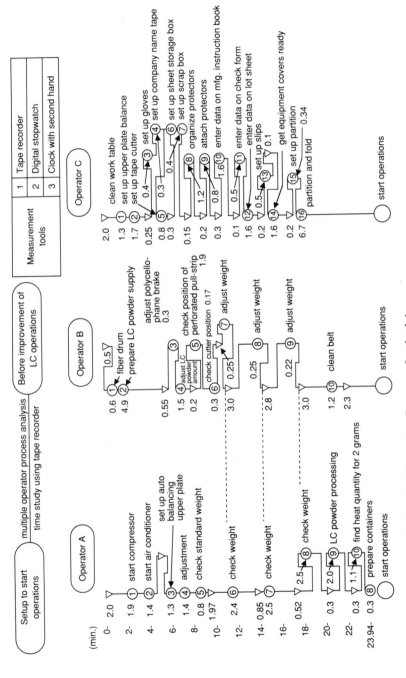

Figure 8-20 Analysis Results (Operator Process Analysis)

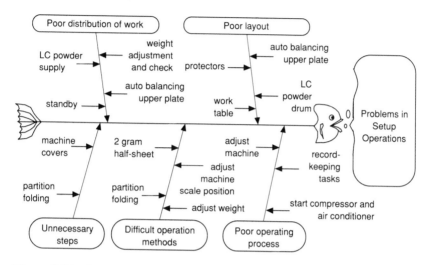

Figure 8-21. Cause-and-effect Diagram of Items from Improvement List

Table 8-6. Main Improvement Measures

Purpose	Item	Measure
Reduce standby	1. Starting air conditioner and compressor	Power supply technician can start air conditioner and compress beforehand
	2. Adjusting and checking weight	One operator can change the balance bar position
Eliminate waste	1. Set up LC powder drum	Move storage site next to machine
	2. Set up containers	Do this the night before
Speed up operations	1. Set up auto balancing upper plate	Mark floor and table to indicate setup positions (horizontal level position)
	2. Calculate the number of half-sheets for 2-gram amounts	Make a quick-reference table to eliminate calculations
	3. Adjust weight	Supply LC powder (as a steady supply) 10 minutes before operation
Other	Overall	1. Eliminate unnecessary steps 2. Clarify operation steps 3. Revise distribution of work with consideration given to mutual timing

Results

Table 8-7 compares the improved setup methods with the previous methods. In a nutshell, these improvements eliminated some of the Big 3 problems from the setup operations and resulted in a 54 percent reduction in setup time. Figure 8-22 shows how the improvement results look when entered into an operator process chart.

Table 8-7. Comparison of Setup Operations Before and After Improvement (Minutes)

		Work	Standby
Operator A	Before improvement	17.6	6.34
	After improvement	11.05	0
Operator B	Before improvement	11.34	12.6
	After improvement	11.05	0
Operator C	Before improvement	20.14	3.8
	After improvement	11.05	0

Overall Results

We also carried out similar analyses and improvement activities for various setup, cleaning, and organizing operations other than the ones just described. In each case our results were at least as good as in this first example. We achieved much of this success after discovering that machine stoppage due to

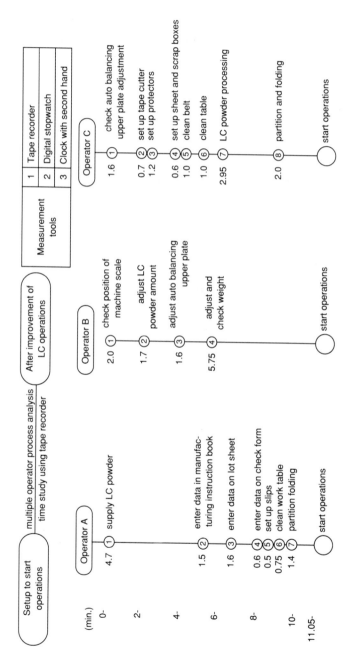

Figure 8-22. Analysis Results After Improvement (Operator Process Analysis)

poor machine conditions was another cause contributing to machine down time. We responded to this by carrying out operating method improvement activities, the effects of which are shown in Figure 8-23.

Effects and Standardization

Effects

1. Tangible effects (see Figure 8-24)
2. Intangible effects
    - The circle members became much more enthusiastic about making improvements (right now we are working on reducing staffing needs).
    - Each person knows what his or her role is and has a stronger sense of participation in the group.
    - Our study sessions helped boost our self-confidence as "can-do" improvement makers.
    - We are looking forward to trying out new work methods (that is our next improvement theme).

Standardization

We revised the operations manual to simplify and clarify the flow of operations.

For the Future

We came up with a motto for our group activities: "Tomorrow is just one step from today." We will not be complacent toward our past successes but will all strive together in future improvement activities.

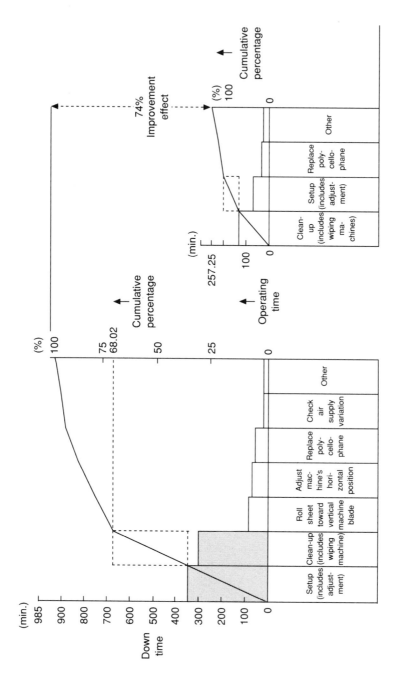

Figure 8-23. Pareto Chart of Conditions Before and After Improvement

		Before Improvement	Target	After Improvement
Higher production output	Day 1	20 kg	35 kg	40 kg
	Day 2 and after	35 kg	42 kg	52 kg
Reduced clean-up time	Last day	140 min.	70 min.	60 min.
Cost savings			¥800,000	¥1,025,000
Activity period			3 mos.	Less than 3 mos.

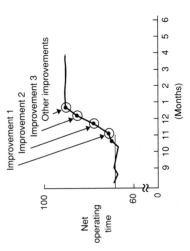

Figure 8-24. Effects

About the Author

Junichi Ishiwata was born in Tokyo in 1926. After graduating from the engineering department of Tokyo University in 1951 with a degree in applied chemistry, he joined NKK Corporation, where he rose to the level of manager of the technology development department. He presently works in the Techno service firm in the technology control department.

Index

OTHER BOOKS ON MANUFACTURING IMPROVEMENT

Productivity Press publishes and distributes materials on continuous improvement in productivity, quality, customer service, and the creative involvement of all employees. Many of our products are direct source materials from Japan that have been translated into English for the first time and are available exclusively from Productivity. Supplemental products and servicee nclude newsletters, conferences, seminars, in-house training and consulting, audio-visual training programs, and industrial study missions. Call 1-800-274-9911 for our free book catalog.

Function Analysis
Systematic Improvement of Quality and Performance
Kaneo Akiyama

As an innovative, flexible company facing new challenges in the 1990s, your organization needs to reexamine continuously the models upon which its operations are based. Function Analysis is a systematic technique for isolating and analyzing various functions in order to better design and improve products. This book gives you a solid understanding of Function Analysis as a tool for system innovation and improvement; it helps you design your products and systems for improved manufacturability and quality. It describes how function analysis is used in the office as well as on the shop floor and.
ISBN 0-915299-81-X / 320 pages / $59.95 / FA-BK

JIT Factory Revolution
A Pictorial Guide to Factory Design of the Future
by Hiroyuki Hirano / JIT Management Library

Here is the first-ever encyclopedic picture book of JIT. With 240 pages of photos, cartoons, and diagrams, this unprecedented behind-the-scenes look at actual production and assembly plants shows you exactly how JIT looks and functions. It shows you how to set up each area of a JIT plant and provides hundreds of useful ideas you can implement. If you've made the crucial decision to run production using JIT and want to show your employees what it's all about, this book is a must. The photographs, from Japanese production and assembly plants, provide vivid depictions of what work is like in a JIT environment. And the text, simple and easy to read, makes all the essentials crystal clear.
ISBN 0-915299-44-5 / 227 pages / $49.95 / Order code JITFAC-BK

Productivity Press, Inc., Dept. BK, P.O. Box 3007, Cambridge, MA 02140 1-800-274-9911

JIT Implementation Manual
The Complete Guide to Just-In-Time Manufacturing

by Hiroyuki Hirano

Here is the most comprehensive and detailed manual we have found anywhere for setting up a complete JIT program. Encyclopedic in scope, and written by a top international consultant, it provides the JIT professional with the answer to virtually any JIT problem. It shows multiple options for handling every stage of implementation and is appropriate to all factory settings, whether in job shop, repetitive, or process manufacturing. Covering JIT concepts, techniques, and tools, and including hundreds of illustrations, charts, diagrams, and JIT management forms, this manual is a truly indispensable tool.
ISBN 0-915299-66-6 / 1000+ pages in 2 volumes / $2500.00 / Order code HIRANO-BK

Kanban and Just-In-Time at Toyota
Management Begins at the Workplace (rev.)

Japan Management Association (ed.), David J. Lu (translator)

Based on seminars developed by Taiichi Ohno and others at Toyota for their major suppliers, this book is the best practical introduction to Just-In-Time available. Now in a newly expanded edition, it explains every aspect of a "pull" system in clear and simple terms — the underlying rationale, how to set up the system and get everyone involved, and how to refine it once it's in place. A groundbreaking and essential tool for companies beginning JIT implementation.
ISBN 0-915299-48-8 / 224 pages / $36.50 / Order code KAN-BK

Canon Production System
Creative Involvement of the Total Workforce

compiled by the Japan Management Association

A fantastic success story! Canon set a goal to increase productivity by three percent per month — and achieved it! The first book-length case study to show how to combine the most effective Japanese management principles and quality improvement techniques into one overall strategy that improves every area of the company on a continual basis. Shows how the major QC tools are applied in a matrix management model.
ISBN 0-915299-06-2 / 251 pages / $36.95 / Order code CAN-BK

Productivity Press, Inc., Dept. BK, P.O. Box 3007, Cambridge, MA 02140 1-800-274-9911

Factory Management Notebook Series
Case Studies in Improvement

Esme McTighe (ed.)

The Factory Management Notebook Series provides subscribers with several notebooks each year of leading-edge articles and case studies translated and compiled from Japan's NKS Factory Management Journal. The Journal has been reporting on new technology and manufacturing breakthroughs for over 15 years. Its authors are among Japan's most renowned industrial leaders and innovators. The Series' first volume (1991) provides fresh information four times throughout the year (six issues are planned for the 1992 volume) on new developments in a specified subject areas: mixed-model production, visual control systems, autonomation/automation, and Total Productive Maintenance (see reverse). For those who would like a "preview" of the series, the notebooks are also offered individually.

Order four-volume set for $600.00.

Mixed-Model Production (Vol.1, No.1) / January 1991 / 184 pages / $175.00 / Order code N1MM-BK

Visual Control Systems (Vol.1, No.2) / April 1991, 200 pages / $175.00 / Order code N1VCS-BK

Autonomation/Automation (Vol.1, No.3) /Summer 1991 / 200 pages / Order code N1AA-BK $175.00

Total Productive Maintenance (Vol.1, No.4) /Fall 1991 / 200 pages / $175.00 / Order code N1TPM-BK

TO ORDER: Write, phone, or fax Productivity Press, Dept. BK, P.O. Box 3007, Cambridge, MA 02140, phone 1-800-274-9911, fax 617-864-6286. Send check or charge to your credit card (American Express, Visa, MasterCard accepted).

U.S. ORDERS: Add $5 shipping for first book, $2 each additional for UPS surface delivery. CT residents add 8% and MA residents 5% sales tax. For each AV program that you order, add $5 for programs with 1 or 2 tapes, and $12 for programs with 3 or more tapes.

INTERNATIONAL ORDERS: Write, phone, or fax for quote and indicate shipping method desired. Pre-payment in U.S. dollars must accompany your order (checks must be drawn on U.S. banks). When quote is returned with payment, your order will be shipped promptly by the method requested.

NOTE: Prices subject to change without notice.

COMPLETE LIST OF TITLES FROM PRODUCTIVITY PRESS

Akao, Yoji (ed.). **Quality Function Deployment: Integrating Customer Requirements into Product Design**
ISBN 0-915299-41-0 / 1990 / 387 pages / $ 75.00 / order code QFD

Asaka, Tetsuichi and Kazuo Ozeki (eds.). **Handbook of Quality Tools: The Japanese Approach**
ISBN 0-915299-45-3 / 1990 / 336 pages / $59.95 / order code HQT

Belohlav, James A. **Championship Management: An Action Model for High Performance**
ISBN 0-915299-76-3 / 1990 / 265 pages / $29.95 / order code CHAMPS

Birkholz, Charles and Jim Villella. **The Battle to Stay Competitive: Changing the Traditional Workplace**
ISBN 0-915-299-96-8 / 1991 / 110 pages / $9.95 /order code BATTLE

Christopher, William F. **Productivity Measurement Handbook**
ISBN 0-915299-05-4 / 1985 / 680 pages / $137.95 / order code PMH

D'Egidio, Franco. **The Service Era: Leadership in a Global Environment**
ISBN 0-915299-68-2 / 1990 / 165 pages / $29.95 / order code SERA

Ford, Henry. **Today and Tomorrow**
ISBN 0-915299-36-4 / 1988 / 286 pages / $24.95 / order code FORD

Fukuda, Ryuji. **CEDAC: A Tool for Continuous Systematic Improvement**
ISBN 0-915299-26-7 / 1990 / 144 pages / $49.95 / order code CEDAC

Fukuda, Ryuji. **Managerial Engineering: Techniques for Improving Quality and Productivity in the Workplace** (rev.)
ISBN 0-915299-09-7 / 1986 / 208 pages / $39.95 / order code ME

Grief, Michel. **The Visual Factory: Building Participation Through Shared Information**
ISBN 0-915299-67-4 / 1991 / 320 pages / $49.95 / order code VFAC

Hatakeyama, Yoshio. **Manager Revolution! A Guide to Survival in Today's Changing Workplace**
ISBN 0-915299-10-0 / 1986 / 208 pages / $24.95 / order code MREV

Hirano, Hiroyuki. **JIT Factory Revolution: A Pictorial Guide to Factory Design of the Future**
ISBN 0-915299-44-5 / 1989 / 227 pages / $49.95 / order code JITFAC

Hirano, Hiroyuki. **JIT Implementation Manual: The Complete Guide to Just-In-Time Manufacturing**
ISBN 0-915299-66-6 / 1990 / 1006 pages / $2500.00 / order code HIRANO

Horovitz, Jacques. **Winning Ways: Achieving Zero-Defect Service**
ISBN 0-915299-78-X / 1990 / 165 pages / $24.95 / order code WWAYS

Japan Human Relations Association (ed.). **The Idea Book: Improvement Through TEI (Total Employee Involvement)**
ISBN 0-915299-22-4 / 1988 / 232 pages / $49.95 / order code IDEA

Japan Human Relations Association (ed.). **The Service Industry Idea Book: Employee Involvement in Retail and Office Improvement**
ISBN 0-915299-65-8 / 1990 / 294 pages / $49.95 / order code SIDEA

Japan Management Association (ed.). **Kanban and Just-In-Time at Toyota: Management Begins at the Workplace** (rev.), Translated by David J. Lu
ISBN 0-915299-48-8 / 1989 / 224 pages / $36.50 / order code KAN

Japan Management Association and Constance E. Dyer. **The Canon Production System: Creative Involvement of the Total Workforce**
ISBN 0-915299-06-2 / 1987 / 251 pages / $36.95 / order code CAN

Jones, Karen (ed.). **The Best of TEI: Current Perspectives on Total Employee Involvement**
ISBN 0-915299-63-1 / 1989 / 502 pages / $175.00 / order code TEI

JUSE. **TQC Solutions: The 14-Step Process**
ISBN 0-915299-79-8 / 1991 / 416 pages / 2 volumes / $120.00 / order code TQCS

Kanatsu, Takashi. **TQC for Accounting: A New Role in Companywide Improvement**
ISBN 0-915299-73-9 / 1991 / 244 pages / $45.00 / order code TQCA

Karatsu, Hajime. **Tough Words For American Industry**
ISBN 0-915299-25-9 / 1988 / 178 pages / $24.95 / order code TOUGH

Karatsu, Hajime. **TQC Wisdom of Japan: Managing for Total Quality Control**, Translated by David J. Lu
ISBN 0-915299-18-6 / 1988 / 136 pages / $34.95 / order code WISD

Kaydos, Will. **Measuring, Managing, and Maximizing Performance**
ISBN 0-915299- 98-4 / 1991 / 208 pages / $34.95 / order code MMMP

Kobayashi, Iwao. **20 Keys to Workplace Improvement**
ISBN 0-915299-61-5 / 1990 / 264 pages / $34.95 / order code 20KEYS

Lu, David J. **Inside Corporate Japan: The Art of Fumble-Free Management**
ISBN 0-915299-16-X / 1987 / 278 pages / $24.95 / order code ICJ

Merli, Giorgio. **Total Manufacturing Management: Production Organization for the 1990s**
ISBN 0-915299-58-5 / 1990 / 224 pages / $39.95 / order code TMM

Mizuno, Shigeru (ed.). **Management for Quality Improvement: The 7 New QC Tools**
ISBN 0-915299-29-1 / 1988 / 324 pages / $59.95 / order code 7QC

Monden, Yasuhiro and Michiharu Sakurai (eds.). **Japanese Management Accounting: A World Class Approach to Profit Management**
ISBN 0-915299-50-X / 1990 / 568 pages / $59.95 / order code JMACT

Nachi-Fujikoshi (ed.). **Training for TPM: A Manufacturing Success Story**
ISBN 0-915299-34-8 / 1990 / 272 pages / $59.95 / order code CTPM

Nakajima, Seiichi. **Introduction to TPM: Total Productive Maintenance**
ISBN 0-915299-23-2 / 1988 / 149 pages / $39.95 / order code ITPM

Nakajima, Seiichi. **TPM Development Program: Implementing Total Productive Maintenance**
ISBN 0-915299-37-2 / 1989 / 428 pages / $85.00 / order code DTPM

Nikkan Kogyo Shimbun, Ltd./Factory Magazine (ed.). **Poka-yoke: Improving Product Quality by Preventing Defects**
ISBN 0-915299-31-3 / 1989 / 288 pages / $59.95 / order code IPOKA

Ohno, Taiichi. **Toyota Production System: Beyond Large-Scale Production**
ISBN 0-915299-14-3 / 1988 / 162 pages / $39.95 / order code OTPS

Ohno, Taiichi. **Workplace Management**
ISBN 0-915299-19-4 / 1988 / 165 pages / $34.95 / order code WPM

Ohno, Taiichi and Setsuo Mito. **Just-In-Time for Today and Tomorrow**
ISBN 0-915299-20-8 / 1988 / 208 pages / $34.95 / order code OMJIT

Perigord, Michel. **Achieving Total Quality Management: A Program for Action**
ISBN 0-915299-60-7 / 1991 / 384 pages / $45.00 / order code ACHTQM

Psarouthakis, John. **Better Makes Us Best**
ISBN 0-915299-56-9 / 1989 / 112 pages / $16.95 / order code BMUB

Robinson, Alan. **Continuous Improvement in Operations: A Systematic Approach to Waste Reduction**
ISBN 0-915299-51-8 / 1991 / 416 pages / $34.95 / order code ROB2-C

Robson, Ross (ed.). **The Quality and Productivity Equation: American Corporate Strategies for the 1990s**
ISBN 0-915299-71-2 / 1990 / 558 pages / $29.95 / order code QPE

Shetty, Y.K and Vernon M. Buehler (eds.). **Competing Through Productivity and Quality**
ISBN 0-915299-43-7 / 1989 / 576 pages / $39.95 / order code COMP

Shingo, Shigeo. **Non-Stock Production: The Shingo System for Continuous Improvement**
ISBN 0-915299-30-5 / 1988 / 480 pages / $75.00 / order code NON

Shingo, Shigeo. **A Revolution In Manufacturing: The SMED System**, Translated by Andrew P. Dillon
ISBN 0-915299-03-8 / 1985 / 383 pages / $70.00 / order code SMED

Shingo, Shigeo. **The Sayings of Shigeo Shingo: Key Strategies for Plant Improvement**, Translated by Andrew P. Dillon
ISBN 0-915299-15-1 / 1987 / 208 pages / $39.95 / order code SAY

Shingo, Shigeo. **A Study of the Toyota Production System from an Industrial Engineering Viewpoint** (rev.)
ISBN 0-915299-17-8 / 1989 / 293 pages / $39.95 / order code STREV

Shingo, Shigeo. **Zero Quality Control: Source Inspection and the Poka-yoke System**,Translated by Andrew P. Dillon
ISBN 0-915299-07-0 / 1986 / 328 pages / $70.00 / order code ZQC

Shinohara, Isao (ed.). **New Production System: JIT Crossing Industry Boundaries**
ISBN 0-915299-21-6 / 1988 / 224 pages / $34.95 / order code NPS

Sugiyama, Tomo. **The Improvement Book: Creating the Problem-Free Workplace**
ISBN 0-915299-47-X / 1989 / 236 pages / $49.95 / order code IB

Suzue, Toshio and Akira Kohdate. **Variety Reduction Program (VRP): A Production Strategy for Product Diversification**
ISBN 0-915299-32-1 / 1990 / 164 pages / $59.95 / order code VRP

Tateisi, Kazuma. **The Eternal Venture Spirit: An Executive's Practical Philosophy**
ISBN 0-915299-55-0 / 1989 / 208 pages/ $19.95 / order code EVS

Yasuda, Yuzo. **40 Years, 20 Million Ideas: The Toyota Suggestion System**
ISBN 0-915299-74-7 / 1991 / 210 pages / $39.95 / order code 4020